DAY BY ORDINARY DAY WITH MARK

DAY BY ORDINARY DAY WITH
M A R K

Daily Reflections for Ordinary Time
Weeks 1-9

VOLUME 1

MARK G. BOYER

ALBA·HOUSE   N E W · Y O R K

SOCIETY OF ST. PAUL, 2187 VICTORY BLVD., STATEN ISLAND, NEW YORK 10314

ST PAULS

Quotations from the New Testament are taken from *The Alba House New Testament*, translated by Mark A. Wauck, copyright © 1997 by the Society of St. Paul, Staten Island, NY. All rights reserved.

Library of Congress Cataloging-in-Publication Data

Boyer, Mark G.
    Day by ordinary day with Mark: daily reflections for ordinary
time / Mark G. Boyer.
       p. cm.
    Contents: v. 1. Weeks 1-9.
    ISBN 0-8189-0783-5
    1. Church year meditations. 2. Bible. N.T. Mark— Meditations.
3. Catholic Church — Prayer-books and meditations — English.
I. Title.
BX2170.C55B72   1997
242'.3 — dc20

                         96-44890
                            CIP

Produced and designed in the United States of America by the
Fathers and Brothers of the Society of St. Paul,
2187 Victory Boulevard, Staten Island, New York 10314,
as part of their communications apostolate.

ISBN: 0-8189-0783-5

Printing Information:

Current Printing - first digit	1	2	3	4	5	6	7	8	9	10

Year of Current Printing - first year shown

1997	1998	1999	2000	2001	2002	2003	2004	2005

Dedicated to my mentor and teacher
Bernard Brandon Scott,
whose great love for the Scriptures
has leavened me.

TABLE OF CONTENTS

Week 7

Week 8

Week 9

Appendix

INTRODUCTION

Today, in Catholic circles there is a strong emphasis on the studying and the praying of the Gospels. In part, this has been brought on by the introduction of the three-year Sunday cycle of Gospel readings and the one-year weekday cycle of Gospel readings in 1974. When a person takes a course, attends a workshop, or participates in a Bible study group, the praying of the Gospels is divorced from the study of the Gospels.

This book attempts to bring such a divorce to an end. This book joins the studying and the praying of the Gospels into a marriage of biblical spirituality that has become the foundation for the Church's proclamation and preaching of the good news during the thirty-three to thirty-four weeks of the liturgical year referred to as Ordinary Time.

According to the "General Norms for the Liturgical Year and the Calendar," issued by the Congregation of Rites in 1969 and revised in 1975, Ordinary Time consists of those thirty-three or thirty-four weeks — distinct from Advent, Christmas, Lent and Easter — "that do not celebrate a specific aspect of the mystery of Christ. Rather... they are devoted to the mystery of Christ in all its aspects" (#43).

Ordinary Time, the longest of all the liturgical seasons, is separated into two parts. The first part usually begins on the Monday after the Sunday Feast of the Baptism of the Lord. In some years, when the Feast of the Baptism of the Lord is celebrated on the Monday following the Solemnity of the Epiphany, Ordinary Time begins on the following Tuesday; the first part ends on the Tuesday before Ash Wednesday.

The second part begins on the Monday after Pentecost Sunday and ends on the evening of the Saturday before the First Sunday of Advent. A Table of Movable Solemnities, Feasts, and Sundays, which is found at the end of this Introduction, will assist the reader in determining the beginnings and endings of the Season of Ordinary Time.

According to the 1981 Introduction to the "Lectionary for Mass," issued by the Sacred Congregation for the Sacraments and Divine Worship, "The Sundays in Ordinary Time do not have a distinctive character. Thus the texts of... the... Gospel readings are arranged in an order of semi-continuous reading" (#67).

Except for the Second Sunday of Ordinary Time, when all three cycles of Gospel selections are from the Gospel according to John, the thirty-three or thirty-four Sundays in Cycle A consist of semi-continuous selections from the Gospel according to Matthew, in Cycle B from the Gospel according to Mark (except for the seventeenth through the twenty-first Sundays and the thirty-fourth Sunday or Solemnity of Christ the King, when selections form the Gospel according to John are read), and in Cycle C from the Gospel according to Luke.

The Introduction to the "Lectionary for Mass" states, "This distribution... provides a certain coordination between the meaning of each Gospel and the progress of the liturgical year. Thus after Epiphany the readings are on the beginning of the Lord's preaching and they fit in well with Christ's baptism and the first events in which He manifests himself. The liturgical year leads quite naturally to a termination in the eschatological theme proper to the last Sundays, since the chapters of the Synoptics that precede the account of the passion treat this eschatological theme rather extensively" (#105).

During some years, particular Solemnities and Feasts which fall on Sundays take precedence over the Sunday in Ordinary Time. These include the Solemnities of the Holy Trinity, the Body and Blood of Christ, the Birth of John the Baptist, Peter and Paul, the Assumption, and All Saints, as well as the Feasts of the Presentation, the Transfiguration, the Triumph of the Cross, the Dedication of St. John Lateran, and All Souls Day. The Gospel readings for these days are found in the Appendix.

The "Lectionary for Mass" also explains that "... the weekday Order of readings is governed by... application of the principles of harmony and of semi-continuous reading" (#69). The semi-continuous reading of the Synoptic Gospels is "arranged in such a way that as the Lord's life and preaching unfold the teaching proper to each of these Gospels is presented" (#105).

During the weekdays of Ordinary Time, the Gospels are arranged so that the Gospel according to Mark is read from the first through the ninth weeks, the Gospel according to Matthew from the tenth through the twenty-first weeks, and the Gospel according to Luke from the twenty-second through the thirty-fourth weeks. The Introduction of the "Lectionary for Mass" explains this schema: "Mark 1-12 are read in their entirety, with the exception only of the two passages of Mark 6 that are read on weekdays in other seasons. From Matthew and Luke the readings comprise all the matters not contained in Mark. From all three Synoptics or from two of them, as the case may be, all those passages are read that are either distinctively presented in each Gospel or are needed for a proper understanding of its progression. Jesus' eschatological discourse as contained in its entirety in Luke is read at the end of the liturgical year" (#109).

The three volumes in this series correspond to the weekday divisions indicated above. Volume I, *Day By Ordinary Day With Mark*, contains the second through the ninth Sundays of Ordinary Time Cycles A, B, and C and the first through the ninth weeks of Ordinary Time, Monday through Saturday. Volume II, *Day by Ordinary Day With Matthew*, contains the tenth through the twenty-first Sundays of Ordinary Time Cycles A, B, and C and the tenth through the twenty-first weeks of Ordinary Time, Monday through Saturday. Volume III, *Day By Ordinary Day With Luke*, contains the twenty-second through the thirty-fourth Sundays of Ordinary Times Cycles A, B, and C and the twenty-second through the thirty-fourth weeks of Ordinary Time, Monday through Saturday.

Each book in this series is designed to be used by individuals for private study of the Gospels and for prayer and by homilists for study of the Gospels, prayer and public preaching. A four-part exercise is offered for every day of the Season of Ordinary Time.

1. A few short verses of Scripture are taken from the Gospel reading provided in the Lectionary for each Mass of each day.

2. A reflective study follows the Scripture selection. The reflection attempts to critique the Gospel selection in light of some contemporary source, form, redaction, literary, and historical criticism. As it offers the individual and the homilist valuable background information concerning the Gospel selection, the reflection yields new perspectives on the Scriptures for personal study and homiletic exegesis in light of contemporary biblical scholarship.

3. The reflection is followed by a question for personal meditation. The question functions as a guide for personal appropriation of the message of the Scripture selection. The homilist can use the question as a basis for a sermon or brief homily.

4. A prayer summarizes the original theme of the Scripture reading, which was studied and explored in the reflection and which served as the foundation for the meditation. The prayer concludes the daily exercise for the individual or it can be used as a fitting conclusion to the General Intercessions and the Liturgy of the Word during the celebration of the Eucharist.

Ordinary Time is the only liturgical season that leaves its mark on all four of the natural seasons of the year. Except for the Solemnity of Christ the King, the last Sunday of Ordinary Time, and a few other Solemnities and Feasts which may interrupt the Ordinary Time Sunday cycles, the color of the season is green. Green, a common color, represents stability, growth, and hope.

The woolen green plaids of January and February in Ordinary Time wrap people in the Winter call of Jesus and the early days of his ministry. The light green of May and June in Ordinary Time are the spring buds of response to Jesus' invitation to experience the kingdom of God. The dark green of July, August, and September in Ordinary Time represent the summer growth in parables, which causes the reader to see the world in different eyes. Finally, the fading green of fall in October and November in Ordinary Time serves as a reminder that the One who once died and was raised will come again.

It is the author's hope that through day by ordinary day study and prayer the reader will come to a deeper knowledge of and a closer relationship with the One around whom all the seasons turn — Jesus, the Christ and Lord.

Mark G. Boyer

TABLE OF MOVABLE SOLEMNITIES, FEASTS, AND SUNDAYS
Volume I
Before Lent

Year	Cycle	Epiphany Jan.	Baptism Jan.	OT begins with wk. 1 on Jan.	OT ends on Tue.	in week #	Feb. 2 replaces OT Sun. #
1997	B	5	12	13	Feb. 11	5	4
1998	C	4	11	12	Feb. 24	7	
1999	A	3	10	11	Feb. 16	6	
2000	B	2	9	10	Mar. 7	9	
2001	C	7	8	9	Feb. 27	8	
2002	A	6	13	14	Feb. 12	5	
2003	B	5	12	.13	Mar. 3	8	4
2004	C	4	11	12	Feb. 24	7	
2005	A	2	9	10	Feb. 8	4	

TABLE OF MOVABLE SOLEMNITIES, FEASTS, AND SUNDAYS
Volume I
After Pentecost

Year	Sun. Cycle	OT begins on Mon.	in week #
1997	B	May 19	7
1998	C	June 1	9
1999	A	May 24	8
2000	B	June 12	10
2001	C	June 1	9
2002	A	May 20	7
2003	B	June 9	10
2004	C	May 31	9
2005	A	May 16	7

DAY BY ORDINARY DAY WITH MARK

CONVERSION

Mark 1:14-20

Monday
of Week

1

Scripture: "The appointed time has come and the kingdom of God is at hand. Repent, and believe in the good news" (Mark 1:15).

Reflection: In three short sentences, Mark's Jesus announces a four-point plan, which will be followed throughout Mark's Gospel.

First, "the time of fulfillment" — as previously prophesied in Mark by John the Baptizer, as predicted by other prophets, and as hoped for by many people — is here. Put in other words, the tree of time now has fruit which is ripe and ready to be picked and eaten.

Second, this ripened fruit is the reign of God. Just as anyone can see that an apple is mature and waiting to be picked, so can anyone be aware of the presence and power of God breaking into the world like a laser flash of light. The "reign of God" is apparent to those who are aware that God is present waiting for us to acknowledge his sovereignty.

Third, reform is important if one is to enter into the kingdom or reign of God. Anyone who reads and/or hears Mark's Gospel is going to be challenged to change his or her life. One's whole outlook and attitude toward life must necessarily be different from that of the world; it will be altered through participation in this Gospel.

1

Fourth, for the reading of this Gospel to be profitable, a person must be willing to say "Amen" to its basic message. An individual must believe in the Gospel, in the good news, which Mark proclaims through the words and deeds of Jesus.

All four points of this plan can be summarized in one single word — conversion. Mark's Gospel is one of conversion.

The first to be converted are Simon and Andrew and James and John. They demonstrate that they are converted by following Jesus. They form the beginning of a long line of witnesses into which every Christian finds himself or herself enrolled.

Meditation: In what ways does your life demonstrate that you have accepted this four-point conversion plan?

Prayer: God of conversion, your Son announced that the time of fulfillment is now, and that your reign is at hand. Equip us with the light of repentance, and strengthen our belief in the Gospel that we may follow Jesus through conversion to new life in the kingdom, where you live with him and the Holy Spirit, one God, for ever and ever. Amen.

TEACHER
Mark 1:21-28

Scripture: Those gathered there were so astonished that they began to argue with one another and say, "What is this? A new teaching presented on his own authority" (Mark 1:27).

Reflection: Mark presents Jesus as a teacher, in fact, as such a good teacher that "the people were astonished at his teaching" (1:22). However, Jesus teaches outside of tradition, where truth is not supposed to exist.

In the Gospel of Mark, Jesus has no past. He simply appears one day while John is baptizing. Jesus is baptized, tempted in the desert, preaches the coming of the kingdom of God, and calls four fishermen to follow him. Then, he begins to teach.

He teaches in his own name, which is a little amazing in Judaism. He teaches with no authority other than his own, which is even more important for the reader to note.

Mark is raising a serious question: Where can one get authority without any tradition to back it up? No wonder, then, the people ask, "What is this?"

Similarly, today, people ask the same question. It may be worded differently, but it is nevertheless the same question. "How do you know that?" one may ask. "Prove it," another may declare. "Who says?" still another may want to know.

It is important to have some authority to support your teaching. However, Mark paints a Gospel-portrait of Jesus as one who has no authority other than his own but teaches nevertheless. "He even gives orders to the unclean spirits, and they obey him." Something important and unusual is going on here. And the people recognize that. Sometimes, truth can be discovered where it is least expected to exist.

Meditation: Who is your favorite teacher? Does he or she teach with authority? Identify his or her authority.

Prayer: God our teacher, you never leave your people unattended. Your Son, Jesus, taught a new way of holiness. Through the work of your Spirit, you continue to write your word of truth upon our hearts. Continue to guide all men and women through the many paths of your truth, so that one day all may share in the eternal life you promise. We ask this through Christ our Lord. Amen.

PRAYER
Mark 1:29-39

Scripture: Early in the morning, long before daylight, Jesus got up, left and went off to a deserted place, where he prayed (Mark 1:35).

Reflection: The modern world is one of a rush to get from one place to the next. It seems that days and months and years pass, and people ask, "Where has the time gone?" People are in a hurry, only to arrive at their destinations to discover that they are in a hurry to get somewhere else.

The Marcan Jesus stands as a statue in the middle of the "Park of Rushing Around." He makes time to pray, for it is in prayer that he discovers his true mission and the means that he must take to be true to it.

Jesus gets up before dawn in order to pray. Here is a simple way to be sure that prayer forms the focus of the day. It takes effort to get up before dawn, but there is something of the divine presence which spills from the light which scatters the darkness of the night.

The place of prayer is important. Mark's Jesus goes into a deserted place. He is alone with no distractions. No desk triggers the day's agenda. No kitchen reminds him of last night's dirty dishes. No newspaper proclaims today's problems. All of these can wait. In a secluded place, the solitude of God can invade a person, and prayer erupts like a volcano.

Meditation: When do you pray? Where do you pray? Do you need to change either?

Prayer: God of the dawn, in the early morning light you spill your life onto your creation. You awaken our spirits to glimpse the glory of your face. Lead us into deserted places, where you can utter your prayer in our hearts. We ask this through our Lord Jesus Christ, your Son, the One who has taught us how to pray, the One who lives with you and the Holy Spirit, one God, for ever and ever. Amen.

TOUCH
Mark 1:40-45

Scripture: "Be made clean" (Mark 1:41).

Reflection: Since the time of Moses, leprosy has been considered a disease which sets a person apart as an outcast. Special places away from the rest of society have been reserved for those with the disease. Such people are treated with nothing that resembles human dignity and respect.

Leprosy, for the most part, is no longer the threat that it once was thanks to the strides in modern medicine. However, the "new leprosy" which threatens society today is AIDS. A new group of people are looked down on and treated as outcasts.

Around the country a few people have manifested the love and wisdom to open homes and shelters for these dying people and to offer them the opportunity to live a few months in peace with human dignity and respect. Those who serve persons with AIDS are like those who cared for the lepers in Jesus' day.

You'll notice that in the Gospel of Mark Jesus was not ashamed or afraid to touch the leper, even though this made him unclean. Such a human-divine gesture was able to heal the leper. Today, a touch of concern for those with AIDS can still accomplish much healing — for the nurse as well as for the patient.

Meditation: Besides those suffering with AIDS, which other groups of people are often treated as outcasts today? Why?

Prayer: God of the suffering, you did not abandon your Son as he hung upon the cross. Do not neglect your people who are in distress today. Send them men and women who are dedicated to your healing work, so that your touch of love may be spread throughout the world. We ask this through Christ our Lord. Amen.

FAITH
Mark 2:1-12

Scripture: And since they couldn't bring him in because of the crowd, they removed the roof above Jesus, and after they had broken through, they lowered the mat on which the paralytic was lying (Mark 2:4).

Reflection: Throughout Mark's Gospel, it is important to notice who is "inside" and who is "outside." It is likewise important to observe carefully who thinks he or she is "inside" and who thinks he or she is "outside." After a while, this inside-outside plot may get confusing, but it is a technique which Mark uses in order to make a point.

And what is this point? Simply stated, it is this: Those who think that they are "inside" often discover that they are really "outside," and those "outside" find that they are really "inside."

In the healing of a paralytic story, Jesus is inside. Around him are gathered many people, but only the scribes are mentioned by name. Of course, the scribes, physically inside, thought of themselves as being "insiders."

The man who is paralyzed is on the "outside." Because of the crowd, he cannot get "inside" the house. So, the faith of those who brought him move them to remove part of the roof and lower him "inside," into the presence of Jesus.

It is important to notice that it is the faith of the paralyzed man and his friends — all of whom are "outside" — which is contrasted to the lack of faith of the scribes — who are supposed to be on the "inside" but in reality are not. The paralyzed man finds himself in more ways than one on the "inside." The story ends upside down.

What is the point that Mark is attempting to make? Those who say they believe may, in fact, not believe, while those who state that they do not believe may by their deeds profess their faith.

Meditation: Do you find that you are "inside" or "outside"?

Prayer: God of paradox, faith is a gift, which you freely give to your people. Strengthen us when we are weak, and enable us to feel your healing power. One day may we come to be "inside" with you, your Son, Jesus, and your Holy Spirit, who live and reign as one God, for ever and ever. Amen.

DOCTOR

Mark 2:13-17

Scripture: "Those who are healthy do not need a physician — the sick do. I came to call sinners, not the righteous" (Mark 2:17).

Reflection: A visit to the doctor's office is made only when a person is ill — or has been sick and is in the process of recovery. Sometimes doctors are visited in order to prevent illness, such as when one has a physical check-up. But, no matter what the specific reason, doctors are usually thought of in terms of helping the sick recover from some kind of illness.

Those considered ill in Mark's Gospel are tax collectors and sinners. Therefore, these two groups of people are in need of a doctor — Jesus.

Levi, son of Alphaeus, is an example of a tax collector, a man who had abandoned the practice of his Jewish faith in order to collect taxes for the Roman occupation forces. Needless to say, the Jews hated tax collectors: for their apostasy, for their association with the Romans, and for the way they made their living — by inflating the amount of the taxes owed and pocketing the difference.

The others who were in need a doctor were the sinners, a polite English word for prostitutes. Of course, this was another despised group, for they, too, made their living by engaging in one of the most repulsive forms of work.

11

These two groups, tax collectors and sinners, needed a doctor. They were the sick, who needed to be healed. These are the people who needed Jesus. They were the ones whom Jesus called.

Mark contrasts the tax collectors and sinners to the Pharisees, the legal-minded, self-righteous group within Judaism. The Pharisees too were called, but they could not bring themselves to respond because of their pride and their prejudiced view of others — the tax collectors and the sinners. They were sick, but they did not know it.

As Mark portrays the situation, Jesus is the doctor for all who were in need of healing. People, however, have to realize that they are sick — as the tax collectors and sinners did. They have to recognize and admit their need for his healing touch. Jesus' office is always open.

Meditation: In what ways are you sick and in need of Jesus' healing?

Prayer: God our healer, you have given us Jesus, our divine physician, to cure us of our sins. Open our hearts and minds to be able to constantly hear his call. May we never become self-righteous and thus feel no need of him, who lives and reigns with you and the Holy Spirit, one God, for ever and ever. Amen.

LAMB OF GOD
John 1:29-34

Scripture: "Behold, the Lamb of God, who takes away the sin of the world" (John 1:29).

Reflection: In John's Gospel, John the Baptizer points out Jesus by referring to him as the "Lamb of God." This title is one which is pregnant with meaning. He does not call Jesus the "Lamb of God" out of mere coincidence.

The annual commemoration of the exodus of the Jews from Egypt where they had been slaves prescribed the use of a lamb, whose blood had once been smeared on the doorposts of the homes of the Israelites. The angel of death "passed over" the homes which were so marked and the lamb became the symbol of life and liberation. The lamb, slaughtered and eaten in a pre-scribed ritual way each year at Passover, triggered the remem-brance of all God's mighty deeds which surrounded their march from slavery to freedom.

It is no accident, then, that John portrays Jesus' death as taking place at the same time as the lambs were being slain in the Temple in preparation for the Passover feast. Jesus, the new lamb, like the Isaian suffering servant led to the slaughter, will pass over from death to life. His blood, like that of the passover lamb, now sets all people free.

Furthermore, Jesus becomes the triumphant lamb, like the

apocalyptic one on the throne in the Book of Revelation. Evil has been destroyed. All people can now pass over from death to life.

Meditation: What is your favorite title for Jesus? What are the various associations it has for you?

Prayer: God our Shepherd, through the blood of a passover lamb, you freed your people from slavery. Through the blood of Jesus, the Lamb of God, you have freed all people from sin and death. Help us to announce your gift of salvation through the lives we lead. We ask this through Christ our Lord. Amen.

RABBI AND MESSIAH

John 1:35-42

Scripture: "What are you looking for?" "We have found the Messiah" (John 1:38, 41).

Reflection: The first two disciples to follow Jesus, according to the Johannine account, are Andrew and, traditionally, John, son of Zebedee, even though John is not mentioned specifically by name. Both Andrew and John are disciples of John the Baptizer. When the Baptist points out Jesus, these two begin to follow him.

The Gospel writer uses two key words in this short account of the meeting of these two disciples and Jesus. In both cases, the writer translates the words so that the reader is sure not to miss their meaning and importance.

First, in response to Jesus' question, "What are you looking for?" Andrew and John address Jesus as "Rabbi," which the evangelist is quick to translate as "Teacher." Throughout the Gospel, Jesus will function as a great rabbi, a great teacher. He will instruct his disciples in the truth and show them the way to life through baptism in water and in the Spirit.

Jesus will teach about the word of life and the bread of life. The new commandment of love will be demonstrated by the unprecedented action of the master (Jesus) washing his disciples' feet. How to inherit eternal life will be a constant theme of his teaching.

Second, once Andrew had found his brother Peter, he tells him, "We have found the Messiah." "Messiah" is the other key word in this Johannine story. The writer quickly reminds the reader that the word "Messiah" means "the Anointed One," "Christ."

Here, however, the writer is interested in stating from the very beginning of the Gospel that Jesus is the one whom the people awaited. Jesus is the person upon whom God has poured out the Spirit; Jesus is the universal Messiah. This becomes clear in the dialogue between Jesus and the Samaritan woman at the well. In the course of their discussion the woman tells Jesus that she knows a "messiah is coming, the one called the Anointed" (4:25). Jesus tells her, "I am he" (4:26).

By the use of these two words, John has laid the foundation for his Gospel. Throughout the rest of the work, he will weave in these words (and many more) to help the reader understand Jesus as the Teacher, who is also the Anointed One of God.

Meditation: In what ways is Jesus "Teacher" and "the Anointed One of God" for you?

Prayer: Father of Jesus, you sent your Son into the world and anointed him with the Spirit in order to teach us the way of eternal life. Help us to always sit attentively at his feet and to learn your way of holiness. We ask this through our Lord Jesus Christ, your Son, who lives and reigns with you and the Holy Spirit, one God, for ever and ever. Amen.

GOOD WINE

John 2:1-12

Scripture: "Everyone serves good wine first, and then when people have drunk freely, an inferior one; but you have kept the good wine until now" (John 2:10).

Reflection: Much of life is made up of a search for the good wine, the best that life can offer. People spend years trying to get the top position in their work, earning and saving money, and raising perfect children. Everyone wants to serve the good wine first.

However, Jesus comes along and, in the Gospel of John, demonstrates that this method of living is all backward. It is the water of life that comes first. Water means beginning at the bottom, being needy and/or poor, and having plenty of human family problems. For most people, this kind of water is to be avoided — like a flood!

What the transformation of water into wine at Cana demonstrates is that only when one is out of wine and has plenty of water can one need Jesus. He transforms emptiness to fullness. He takes the water of life and turns it into the best wine. In this way, the best wine is saved until last. Instead of avoiding the watery times, people should celebrate them. By immersing themselves into the water, they emerge as wine. The transformation occurs daily for those who can see. And every time it happens, people can see the glory of Jesus and believe in him.

Meditation: What recent water-experience was turned into wine for you?

Prayer: God of water and wine, you flood the earth with your presence and give us to drink of the Holy Spirit. Continue to bless us with your many gifts. Lead us through the water of life to the wine of eternal life. We ask this through Christ our Lord. Amen.

BRIDEGROOM
Mark 2:18-22

Scripture: "Can the groomsmen fast while the bridegroom is with them? As long as the bridegroom is with them they cannot fast" (Mark 2:19).

Reflection: A metaphor is an implied comparison of one thing to another. Jesus in today's passage from Mark's Gospel, employs the marriage metaphor, specifically the bridal dimension, to emphasize the deep personal love relationship between God and his people.

In the person of Jesus, God is the bridegroom who desires to be with his bride, his people. At such a moment there can be no fasting — a practice of the Pharisees and a sign of self-denial out of love. Fasting would get in the way of this initial intimate union between God and his people.

To fast during a marriage feast would be as ridiculous as sewing a new piece of denim onto old blue jeans. After the first washing, the patch would shrink and pull away from the jeans, leaving a larger hole than before.

Likewise, to fast during a marriage feast would be as senseless as putting new wine into old wineskins. The gases formed by the new wine would enlarge the old skins and cause them to explode; thus, both wine and skins would be lost. New wine needs new, strong skins to be stored properly.

There are times for both feasting and fasting. When people, the bride, celebrate their nuptial relationship with God, the bridegroom, they feast. However, as in any marriage, after the honeymoon is over and they have grown deeper and more fully into their relationship with one another, they will find ample opportunity and reason to fast.

Meditation: How often do you feast? How often do you fast?

Prayer: God our bridegroom, we, your bride, celebrate your constant presence among us with a feast. Draw us more closely to yourself. Through our times of fasting, help us to enter more deeply into that relationship which you share with your Son, Jesus, and your Holy Spirit, one God, for ever and ever. Amen.

MEETING NEEDS

Mark 2:23-28

Scripture: "Haven't you ever read what David did when *he* was in need and he and his companions were hungry?" (Mark 2:25).

Reflection: What is more important: keeping the rules of the Sabbath (today, Sunday) or meeting the needs of the people? While this question is an old one, it is one that, nevertheless, needs constant answering.

Oftentimes, it is easier to keep the rules than to meet human needs. Mark's Pharisees are portrayed as rule keepers; they point out to Jesus that his disciples break the Sabbath rule by picking heads of grain.

Jesus in Mark's Gospel quickly points out that genuine human need takes precedence over the rules governing human life and conduct. David and his men broke the rules in order to satisfy their hunger; the very real needs of people are more important than rules.

The purpose of the Sabbath — rest — was to imitate God, who after six days of creating took time out for a break. As Jesus states it, the Sabbath was made for the people. It is God's gift to them.

To turn it around and say that people were made for the Sabbath is to get it backward. People are not made to fit rules;

rules are made to fit the needs of people. When rules no longer serve their purpose, then they are to be changed, abolished or ignored.

So often people cling to the rules because rules offer safety, security, and protection from change. However, such an enclosure does not necessarily serve their needs. When someone is hungry, no rule concerning the proper time for meals is appropriate — as demonstrated by David and Jesus.

Likewise, when someone is sick, no rule concerning the usual office hours of a doctor applies. When someone has been in an accident and is being rushed to the hospital, the rule about stopping at every red light no longer applies in deference to the suffering person. Common sense and prudent judgment, rather, must prevail.

Meditation: Do you place rules above people or people above rules?

Prayer: God of the Sabbath, you give us laws and rest that we might serve you and our brothers and sisters better. Through your Holy Spirit keep us balanced; give us a great appreciation for your Law, but also give us eyes to see people in need. We ask this through our Lord Jesus Christ, your Son, the Lord of the Sabbath, who lives and reigns with you and the Holy Spirit, one God, for ever and ever. Amen.

HEALING
Mark 3:1-6

Scripture: The man held out his hand and it was restored (Mark 3:5).

Reflection: Throughout the first half of his Gospel, Mark portrays Jesus as an exorcist, a miracle-worker, and a healer. He portrays Jesus as a man with divine power. Later in the Gospel, after the scene with Peter near Caesarea Philippi, Mark will show another characteristic of Jesus and present him as the rejected, suffering, and abandoned Son of Man.

In the story of the man with a withered hand, Jesus' display of power, while in the presence of the Pharisees and the Herodians and on the Sabbath, is more subtle. Mark never tells us that Jesus did anything except to tell the man to hold out his hand.

In the world today, much healing can take place if people are just willing to reach out a hand to another person. The mother with children who seem to be constant problems can be healed by another, usually an older, woman who is willing to give a hand to help, to baby-sit, or to simply hold the other's hand and listen.

A few hours spent with a friend can be another way that one offers a hand to another. Sometimes a helping hand takes the form of a confrontation, a severe telling of the truth in love, which enables a person to see himself or herself more clearly.

Every day presents opportunities for people to give and to receive a hand from one another.

Much healing can be brought into the world this way.

Meditation: To whom have you recently stretched out your hand? Who has recently stretched out a hand to you?

Prayer: God of healing, in the person of Jesus, your Son, you have stretched out your healing hand to the human race. With the help of your Spirit enable us to reach out and grasp his hand and thus come to share in your eternal life. We ask this through Christ our Lord. Amen.

SON OF GOD
Mark 3:7-12

Scripture: As soon as the unclean spirits saw him they'd fall down before him and cry out, "You are the Son of God" (Mark 3:11).

Reflection: One of the ways that Mark characterizes Jesus is as an exorcist, one who gets rid of unclean spirits. It is important to note that an unclean spirit is not equivalent to what today might be referred to as demonic possession. For Mark, any ailment — physical, psychological, emotional, etc. — that cannot be understood is an unclean spirit.

Also, these so-called unclean spirits always know who Jesus is and call him "Son of God." Mark continually contrasts the unclean spirits to the disciples, who should know who Jesus is but never seem to figure it out.

In the first half of Mark's Gospel, the designation "Son of God" by the unclean spirits is contrasted to the designation "Son of Man" in the second half of the Gospel. "Son of God" indicates power — the kind which is greater than that of the unclean spirits, although there is never any "contest" between Jesus and the unclean spirits; they simply acknowledge defeat.

"Son of Man" also indicates power, but it is power of a different kind. In the second half of Mark's Gospel, Jesus' power is made manifest in his powerlessness. Authentic power is found in weakness.

For Christians to call Jesus "Son of God" is to declare one kind of power, a type which Jesus in the Gospel of Mark clearly rejects. To refer to Jesus as "Son of Man" is to indicate a kind of power which stems from powerlessness. It is in weakness — rejection, suffering, and death — that God's power reaches perfection.

Meditation: How in your life have you experienced the power of the "Son of God"? In how many more ways in your life have you experienced the power of the "Son of Man"? Which was more effective?

Prayer: God of power, it was not in your Son's victory over unclean spirits that you designated him as Savior, but it was in his rejection, suffering and death. Help us to understand this mystery of your love. Trace in us the lines of your powerlessness that we may share completely in the life of your Godhead: Father, Son, and Holy Spirit, one God, for ever and ever. Amen.

MOUNTAIN

Mark 3:13-19

Scripture: Then he went up the mountain and called those whom he wanted and they came to him (Mark 3:13).

Reflection: Any time anything is portrayed as taking place on a mountain, the reader is being invited by the writer to take notice. So, when Mark situates Jesus on a mountain and Jesus summons and appoints the twelve (another text marker), the writer wants the reader to focus on this part of the Gospel.

In order to get the point, three clues need to be considered. First, a mountain is a place of God's self-revelation. Moses received the Law on a mountain. Later, in Mark's account, Jesus will be transfigured on a mountain with both Moses and Elijah being present.

Second, "the twelve" indicate the beginning of a new group of people. It was out of the federation of the twelve tribes of Israel that God initially formed for himself a people. From these twelve (otherwise called apostles), Jesus will form for himself a new group of believers.

Also, since Mark portrays Jesus as a type of "warrior," he needs "soldiers," who will join him in battle. Therefore, three times in the first six chapters of his Gospel, Mark portrays the call and the missioning of the disciples.

Third, only Mark calls his work a "Gospel." "Gospel" is not a religious term; it is a political one. Literally, it means good news, and often is used to refer to the message regarding a victory in battle; the enemy has been defeated.

By calling his work a "Gospel," Mark is expanding the meaning of the word to cover the whole of the life of Jesus, and he is foretelling the victory that is connected to his theological narrative about Jesus. In a way, Mark's Gospel is an extended homily, an act of preaching, a proclamation of "good news."

When these clues — the mountain, the twelve, and the Gospel — are all combined, the reader should be inclined to ask certain questions: What is the victory? Where is the victory to take place? Who will enable the victory to take place? Who is the victor? These are precisely the questions the writer wished to arouse in the hope that the reader would continue to look for the answers in his work.

Meditation: In what situations has God revealed himself to you? With whom did you share this "Gospel"?

Prayer: God of the mountain, in times past you gave your law to Moses and your guidance to Elijah. In the person of Jesus, your servant and your Son, you have revealed the vastness of your love. Help us to follow him through suffering and death to a victorious new life with you. We ask this through the same Christ our Lord. Amen.

FAMILY
Mark 3:20-21

Scripture: "He's out of his mind" (Mark 3:21).

Reflection: For most people the thought of their family causes a warm, cozy feeling to well up inside. Family means security; in a family a person is accepted as he or she is.

Jesus' family, however, thinks that he is "out of his mind" (3:21). When he comes home, they attempt to seize him as Mark narrates the story. For Jesus, family does not represent secure acceptance, but it becomes an occasion for rejection.

Mark portrays Jesus' family's rejection of him as a foretaste of what will take place by all Jesus' followers later in the Gospel. For Mark, rejection is an important dimension of discipleship. Rejection is not a word that most people like to hear.

Rejection and family do not fit together. And this is exactly the point Mark is trying to make, and one which will be fleshed out in detail a little later in this same chapter.

Those who seem to be in the inner circle (family) are offered the same opportunity to accept or reject Jesus as those outside his inner circle. They have it no easier than those who are on the outside. In other words, discipleship is offered and opened to all.

Meditation: To what different families do you belong? How do you live discipleship in each?

Prayer: God of all families, you sent Jesus, your Son, who was born into the human family. Give us the wisdom to follow his way of discipleship. We ask this through our Lord Jesus Christ, who lives and reigns with you and the Holy Spirit, one God, for ever and ever. Amen.

LIGHT

Matthew 4:12-23

Scripture: "The people living in darkness have seen a great light, and on those living in the land and shadow of death a light has dawned" (Matthew 4:16).

Reflection: When Jesus begins his Galilean ministry, as Matthew narrates the story, he leaves Nazareth and goes to live in Capernaum, where Matthew portrays him as fulfilling Isaiah's prophecy of a great light dawning upon Zebulun and Naphtali. This theme of light is an important dimension of the first part of Matthew's Gospel, especially in helping us comprehend how he understands Jesus as being the Savior of the Gentiles.

According to Matthew, the first visitors to the infant Jesus are magi from the East. The East was considered the place of darkness, for it was in the East that Babylon was located. In Babylon the Israelites had been captive, prisoners of war, for seventy years. In his typical irony, Matthew brings in pagan Gentiles from this area to worship the newborn child.

Furthermore, they follow a light, a star. When they get to the city of light, Jerusalem, the star is lost. When they leave the city, they find it again. Matthew is proclaiming the acceptance of the star, Jesus, by the Gentiles and his rejection by his own people.

Therefore, after his baptism and temptation in the desert,

Matthew has Jesus begin his ministry — not to the Jews — but to the Gentiles. The echo of the magi story is heard in the words about a people living in darkness and seeing a great light. Jesus is the great light, who dawns on all people — Jew and Gentile alike.

He proclaims the nearness of the kingdom of heaven and calls the first disciples, Peter and Andrew, James and John, to follow him. Thus Matthew portrays the beginning of Jesus' ministry of light to the Gentiles.

Meditation: In what ways has Jesus been a great light for you?

Prayer: God of light, you never abandon your people to the night. When we are in the darkness, you shine the light of hope of Jesus on us. Move us to repent, for the kingdom of heaven, where you live with your Son, our Lord Jesus Christ, and the Holy Spirit, is at hand. You are God for ever and ever. Amen.

HERALD
Mark 1:14-20

Scripture: After John was arrested, Jesus came into Galilee proclaiming the good news of God (Mark 1:14).

Reflection: Mark's Gospel, like the other Gospels, portrays John the Baptist as the Isaian messenger who prepares the way for Jesus. Since his role is that of a precursor, he has to be removed from the scene before Jesus begins his public Galilean ministry. Mark simply tells the reader that John was arrested.

It is important to note how quickly and without mention of detail all this takes place. John appears baptizing. Jesus comes to the Jordan and is baptized by John. Jesus goes into the desert, where he is tempted. Then he begins his public ministry by announcing that the kingdom of God is at hand and calling his first disciples. All this takes place in the first twenty verses of the first chapter of Mark's Gospel.

It is only later in chapter six of the Gospel that the reader discovers that it was Herod who had arrested John. The details of the situation surrounding the Baptist's death are given — details which prefigure the death of Jesus.

In the early Church, the role of the Baptizer caused some problems. If John baptized Jesus, then, according to the thinking of the time, the greater of the two must logically be the one administering the baptism. Matthew tried to finesse this problem by portraying John as declining to baptize Jesus, until Jesus insists that John do it. Luke solved the problem by placing John in prison before mentioning the baptism of Jesus; he doesn't say who was responsible for his baptism. In John's Gospel, it is clear that Jesus is the pre-existent Word and much greater than John. He doesn't say that John the Baptizer baptized Jesus, but has John mention having seen the descent of the Holy Spirit upon Jesus during the period when he was baptizing with water.

No matter how the Baptizer is portrayed in the Gospels, his role is always the same: to prepare the way of the Lord. Today, this function belongs to all people. Every person is responsible for making the way straight for the Lord to come into his or her own life and into the life of the community.

The voice of the herald of good news (John) can still be heard, if men and women are willing and ready to speak in his stead.

Meditation: In what ways do you function as a John the Baptizer today?

Prayer: God of Jesus, through your prophet John, you heralded the good news of your Son's coming. Through the waters of baptism, you enabled John to prepare the way. You have called us through the rivers of baptism to continue to prepare the way for Jesus to come into the hearts of all men and women. Guide us in our work: be the words we speak and the good news we live. We ask this through Christ our Lord. Amen.

PERSONAL GOSPEL

Luke 1:1-4; 4:14-21

Scripture: It seemed proper that I, too, after carefully ex-
amining everything anew, should write you an orderly account, so that you may recognize the certainty of the words
concerning which you have been instructed (Luke 1:3-4).

Reflection: Luke's Gospel is the only one of the synoptic Gospels (Matthew, Mark, and Luke) to begin with a prologue, four
verses which introduce his Gospel narrative. Such a prologue is
a literary device, which imitates Hellenistic writing. By employing the prologue, Luke places his work in the general world of
literature.

In the prologue the author tells the reader what he will do
in the narrative — create an orderly sequence of events after careful investigation. This is equivalent to writing a book after doing
research.

One point to be gleaned from the prologue is the fact that
the ordering of the events is based on Luke's researched understanding of them for the purpose of teaching. This means that his
narrative will be based on his theological perspective. This narrative will be different from those that preceded it insofar as its
author is preparing his work for a specific audience who live in
a particular part of the world during a definite time.

He is not writing a biography, a chronicle, or a work of history. He is preparing a theological narrative, whose characters, scenes, and plot reveal an answer to the questions: Who is Jesus? What does Jesus means now (when the book was written)? In other words, to understand the narrative, some information needs to be known about the audience, their location in the world, and the time they existed. These give clues to the theological position of Luke's narrative.

Most people possess their own mental composite of the good news which is made up of bits and pieces from all the Gospels.

Such a "personal Gospel" could never have canonical status — even though it does possess a definite theological position! There are only four canonical (and many non-canonical) Gospels, which means that there are four official (and many non-official) ways of answering: Who is Jesus? What does Jesus mean now?

Meditation: What does your "personal, mental Gospel" look like? Write an outline of it without consulting any of the official Gospels.

Prayer: God of writers, you inspired your servant, Luke, to prepare a written narrative of the events of your Son, Jesus. Through his work continue to inspire and teach us. Enable us to grow in your wisdom and your grace. We ask this through our Lord Jesus Christ, who lives and reigns with you and the Holy Spirit, one God, for ever and ever. Amen.

DIVISION
Mark 3:22-30

Scripture: "If a kingdom is divided against itself, that kingdom cannot stand. And if a house is divided against itself, that house will be unable to stand" (Mark 3:24-25).

Reflection: When something is divided, it is weakened. Saw off part of one of the legs on a table, and the table's stability teeter-totters. Separate a group of ten people into smaller groups of five each, and the force is divided. If a leg or an arm is broken, the whole body of the person is weakened.

Because Mark strongly portrays Jesus as an exorcist, he has to deal with the problem that some people believed that Jesus himself was not only possessed by an unclean spirit (anything not "scientifically" explainable), but that it was in the name of evil that he exorcised. Put simply, what Mark presents is a refutation of the "two super powers" understanding of the world.

The two super powers did not consist of the Soviet Union and the United States. Rather, the super powers were considered to be God and Satan who were equals in every sense of the word. To think in such terms is to place the world in jeopardy — not to mention what it does to the biblical understanding of the one good God, who creates everything out of nothing — including Satan who is in no way his equal — and forms people in his own image and likeness.

What Jesus illustrates is that there are not two super powers. There is only one: God! Jesus, undoubtedly known in Marcan circles as an exorcist, relies on God's power to heal. He states the obvious: he cannot be possessed by an unclean spirit or drive out demons in the name of the prince of demons, for to do so would divide the "force" of evil, which would mean that it has demolished itself.

Two analogies are given to make the point. A divided kingdom is easily conquered. A divided family loses its resistance to the thief. Similarly, if Jesus were possessed or healed in the name of evil, he would be toppling himself. Jesus heals through the power and work of the Holy Spirit.

The kingdom of God is strengthened by Jesus' exorcisms, Mark is saying. There are not two super powers; there is only one, and he is God. The reader must remember that Jesus' first line in this Gospel is: "The appointed time has come. The kingdom of God is at hand" (Mark 1:15).

Meditation: In what ways have you found yourself divided and, therefore, weakened? Where do you find your strength?

Prayer: God of the kingdom, through Jesus, your servant and your Son, you continue to heal a broken world. Where there is division, bring unity; where there is hatred, bring love; where there is war, bring peace. Bring us one day to the kingdom where you live and reign with your Son, our Lord Jesus Christ, and your Holy Spirit, one God, for ever and ever. Amen.

DOING THE WILL OF GOD

Mark 3:31-35

Scripture: "…Whoever does the will of God is my brother and sister and mother" (Mark 3:35).

Reflection: In the account of Jesus' mother and brothers arriving in order to see him and, most probably, to take him away because they thought he was "out of his mind" (3:21), Mark intentionally places Jesus' relatives outside of the place where Jesus is, and he places the crowd inside with Jesus. It is important to remember here that "inside" and "outside" are important places for Mark.

By setting up the scene in this way, Mark is arguing that salvation is not genetic; salvation is not found in the proper "blood line." A person does not get "inside" by belonging to the right group; it does not matter if that group be tribe, family, or "crowd."

Also, Mark does not want family members to have any special claim in the story. He is interested in showing that faith is not passed on because one happens to be a member of a particular family, but because a person is converted.

Therefore, Jesus' family members are "outside." They are quickly presented and then removed from the scene. They have no further part to play in the Marcan plot.

The authentic family of Jesus consists of anyone who does

the will of God. The individual who does God's will is either a brother, a sister, or a mother of Jesus.

Meditation: In what ways have you discovered that you are a brother, a sister, or a mother of Jesus?

Prayer: God our Father, to the family of humankind you sent your Son and our brother, Jesus. Through his life and death, he showed us that all men and women are brothers and sisters. By doing your will may we be drawn even more closely into the circle of the love you share with your Son and the Holy Spirit, one God, for ever and ever. Amen.

IN PARABLES

Mark 4:1-20

Scripture: Then he taught them many things in parables...
"To you is given the secret of the kingdom of God, but to
those outside everything is given in parables, so that 'although they look, they may see yet not perceive, and
though they listen, they may hear yet not understand,' lest
they be converted and find forgiveness" (Mark 4:2, 11-12).

Reflection: Most of the fourth chapter of Mark's Gospel is a sermon of parables by Jesus. This particular section of the Gospel is
an interlude that stops the action which was begun in the preceding three chapters: the rejection of Jesus by the Pharisees and
their plotting his death, the placement of Jesus' family on the
"outside," and the attraction of the crowd to Jesus.

For Mark, parables function as riddles; this means that they
have some secret explanation. Those who understand the riddle
are "inside" the kingdom of God, while those who fail to comprehend are on the "outside" — they hear but do not understand.

Oftentimes, those on the "outside" believe that they see and
hear, but they do not. Jesus can be seen and heard, according to
Mark, and totally misunderstood.

The real riddle of the kingdom of God is why people ap-
parently believe but do not persevere. Faithfulness is the issue.
In Mark's understanding, faithfulness means perseverance. Only
some people persevere, however.

Mark is addressing the reader, who believes himself or herself to be faithful. The central mystery of faith is that people fall away; this is the paradoxical riddle. The seed is sown everywhere, but each grain does not bear fruit. In fact, three-fourths of the seed produces no grain at all.

The issue of faithfulness — in terms of perseverance — is a riddle with which every Christian must grapple. Otherwise, he or she may think that he or she is "inside" only to discover that he or she is really "outside." "Whoever has ears to hear, let them hear" (Mark 4:9).

Meditation: How do you characterize your faithfulness — in terms of perseverance: seed on the path, seed on rocky ground, seed among thorns, seed on rich soil? Why?

Prayer: God of parables, through the riddles of Jesus, your Son, you have revealed the mystery of your kingdom. Enable us to see and to perceive, to hear and to understand in order that we may be converted and be forgiven. We ask this through our Lord Jesus Christ, who lives and reigns with you and the Holy Spirit, one God, for ever and ever. Amen.

HIDDEN MADE VISIBLE
Mark 4:21-25

Scripture: "Nothing is hidden unless it is to be revealed; nothing is covered up unless it is later to be brought into the open" (Mark 4:22).

Reflection: The parable of the lamp re-emphasizes Mark's point already made in the first part of Jesus' sermon in chapter four: riddles reveal the mystery of the kingdom of God. This particular riddle uses the image of light.

Light was a precious resource in the ancient world. It usually took the form of an oil lamp, which would give little light in comparison to modern electric light standards. The lamp was placed on a stand so that an optimum amount of its light could be used.

Therefore, when the Marcan Jesus asks about putting it under a bushel basket or under a bed, the crowd has to break out into laughter. The thought was ridiculous; the action would make no sense. It would be a waste of light.

Parables function as a lamp for Mark; they reveal what is hidden about the kingdom; they shine into the darkest corners and uncover its secrets. For those who know how to use a lamp (parable) properly, knowledge and experience of the kingdom of God is granted.

Meditation: What has been your most recent insight or experience of God? How was this like light?

Prayer: God of light, through Jesus, your servant and your Son, you announced the good news of your kingdom. Through the gift of your Holy Spirit, light our way and direct our steps. Help us to understand and see what great things you have prepared for us. We ask this through Christ our Lord. Amen.

SEED
Mark 4:26-34

Scripture: "This is how the kingdom of God is; it is like a man who scatters seed upon the earth and sleeps and rises by night and day, and the seed sprouts and grows while he is unaware" (Mark 4:26-27).

Reflection: The parable of the seed growing by itself is found only in Mark's Gospel. The growth of seed is no great surprise to people today. The planting, the growing, and the harvesting are no longer great mysteries.

However, to ancient people, the scattering, the sprouting, the growing, and the resulting fruit were mysterious, as they did not have the biological knowledge which is available today. A biological understanding of germination and fruition does not necessarily remove the mystery or negate the parable.

The parable is about the kingdom of God, which grows without human intervention. The fruition of the kingdom is not dependent on people, for it is all God's doing through Jesus, the proclaimer of the kingdom. The kingdom will continue its silent and slow growth until the day of the harvest, the apocalyptic end of the world.

The point that Mark is attempting to make by relating this parable is this: faith should yield more faith. In other words, the faith of one person should keep growing; there is never a time to stop. As faith continues to grow, so does the kingdom of God.

Just as the seed draws its life and nourishment from the soil, so the individual believer must draw his or her life and nourishment from prayer, the Scriptures, the sacraments, etc. These cannot become routine; otherwise, the growing stops. Growing in faith is a life-long endeavor; it is only at the moment of death that the individual grain is ripe and ready for the harvester. Throughout the growth, however, a person is unknowingly spreading the kingdom of God.

Meditation: What means have you taken to be sure that you continue to grow in faith and do not find yourself stuck in a routine?

Prayer: God of the harvest, you scatter the seed of your kingdom in the lives of your people. Throughout the days and nights it sprouts and grows and reaches fruition. Send your Holy Spirit as our guide, so that we may produce abundantly and come to share in the fullness of your kingdom, where you live and reign with Jesus Christ, your Son, in the unity of the Holy Spirit, one God, for ever and ever. Amen.

ORDER OUT OF CHAOS

Mark 4:35-41

Scripture: Then he woke up and rebuked the wind and said to the sea, "Be still!" (Mark 4:39).

Reflection: Scripture scholars refer to the account of the stilling of the storm at sea as a nature miracle. In the Jewish mindset the sea was the place of chaos. It was out of the chaos that God brought order in the Book of Genesis.

Likewise, in this narrative of the calming of the sea, Jesus brings order out of chaos. This is Mark's story — his theology; he is telling the reader who Jesus is by the way Jesus acts. He is one who brings order out of chaos, who calms the storms of life.

This, of course, is not the only instance of order being brought forth from chaos. The same, simple phrase ("Be still!"), which is used to quiet the sea, is also used to silence an unclean spirit (1:25).

What Mark is emphasizing is the power of the spoken word. The reader must remember that the incident of calming the sea occurs immediately after Jesus' sermon, which consists of several parables each comparing the kingdom of God to some other reality. Just as the parable has the ability to make a person aware of the presence of the kingdom of God, so too do the simple words addressed to the sea.

For Mark, the word is meant to evoke faith. In the healing

and the cleansing stories and in the parables, faith is emphasized. Likewise, in the nature miracle, the point is faith. After the sea is calmed, Jesus asks those in the boat with him, "Why are you so afraid? Do you not yet have faith?" (4:40).

The disciples of Jesus, as portrayed by Mark throughout the Gospel, never believe. This is important to note because Mark does not think that healings and miracles are reasons to believe. Therefore, any healings or miracles that the disciples witness do not lead them to faith. For Mark, the spoken word of Jesus should be enough for a person to believe.

Meditation: Do you believe because of healings and miracles, or do you believe because you heard the word of God? Explain.

Prayer: God of the sea, out of the chaos of the beginning you fashioned the earth and every living thing upon it. You brought forth order and beauty by the work of your hands. Through Jesus you re-fashioned the world and all the people in it. May his word resound in our ears and move our hearts to a deeper faith in you, who live and reign with Jesus and the Holy Spirit, one God, for ever and ever. Amen.

BLESSEDNESS

Matthew 5:1-12

SUNDAY
of Week

4

Cycle A

Scripture: "Blessed are the poor in spirit, for theirs is the kingdom of heaven" (Matthew 5:3).

Reflection: Chapter five of Matthew's Gospel begins with Jesus going up a mountain and teaching the disciples. In this portrayal, Matthew obviously understands Jesus to be a new Moses.

Furthermore, the first teaching of chapter five consists of the beatitudes, which introduce the first of five (like the five books of Moses) great sermons in Matthew's Gospel. This first sermon occupies all of chapters five, six, and seven.

The nine Matthean beatitudes all begin with the word "blessed." To be "blessed" is to share in the characteristics of God. In its root sense, the word means to be "happy"; it is that characteristic which puts a person at ease.

In each beatitude there is an inherent contradiction between the wished-for happiness and the state of the person described. Thus, it is a language of excess or hyperbole. It challenges the reader to bring together contradictions and to see a new vision through such a paradox.

For instance, the first beatitude declares happy those who are poor in spirit. Rephrased, this is equivalent to saying, "How content are those who are psychologically devastated!" "How fantastic it is for those who are depressed!" These experiences, which are usually viewed as negative by most people, are opportunities for one to sense the need and, hence, experience the presence of God.

Those who have achieved everything and finished looking like God are those who depend on God for everything. They already have the kingdom of heaven now. Of course, it takes great faith to understand the truths which lie beneath the surface of the paradoxes we find in the Gospels: that it is in giving that we receive, in pardoning that we are pardoned and in dying that we are born to eternal life.

The point is this: happiness (blessedness) cannot be achieved or earned or worked for. It is a gift of God which he freely bestows on those with faith. Happiness is already given to people now; they can experience the kingdom of God now. Where? In the very experiences which are usually looked upon as negative is where God is found. Because of Jesus, every experience of life bears the potential of happiness. In Jesus, the paradox is fulfilled.

Meditation: When have you most recently experienced happiness (blessedness) while being sad or depressed (poor in spirit)? Did you discover God in this experience?

Prayer: Blessed are you, God of the poor in spirit. In the most painful experiences of our lives you manifest your kingdom. Through our humanness we come to be like you. In Jesus, we are able to recognize you in our human flesh. Continue to teach us your ways. We ask this through our Lord Jesus Christ, your Son, who lives and reigns with you and the Holy Spirit, one God for ever and ever. Amen.

MESSIANIC SECRET

Mark 1:21-28

Scripture: "What do you want with us, Jesus of Nazareth? Have you come to destroy us? I know who you are — the Holy One of God!" (Mark 1:24)

Reflection: Throughout Mark's Gospel, there exists a theme, which is often referred to as the "messianic secret." What this refers to is the fact that Jesus in this Gospel often exhorts those with whom he comes into contact not to tell others about him.

Ironically, the "messianic secret" seems to be known by everyone in the Gospel who should not know it, whereas those who should know who the Messiah is do not ever seem to recognize him. So, unclean spirits cry out that Jesus is the Son of God, a title which was used only in the first verse of the Gospel and by the voice from the heavens in a private moment following Jesus' baptism and transfiguration.

This pattern will continue to be seen throughout the rest of the Gospel. The unclean spirits, the outcasts, those who should not know who Jesus is will constantly be proclaiming the truth while those who should be able to identify him, the disciples, never seem to get it.

In presenting scenes like this, Mark is trying to alert his readers. So often people think they know who Jesus is, and what it means to call him "Messiah," "Son of God," and "Lord." Mark is stating that such people may find out that this is not enough. Jesus recognizes as his own only those who hear his word and keep it. To the others he will say, "I do not know you."

The turning point, the clearest statement of this theme, will be found near the end of chapter eight of the Gospel. Here, Mark makes perfectly clear that "Messiah," "Son of God," and "Lord" have to do with power, in which Jesus is not interested.

A new title is given to Jesus — "Son of Man." This title indicates that Jesus is the suffering, dying, and rising Messiah; he is powerless. Those who think that following a Jesus of power is the way of discipleship, according to Mark, quickly discover that they do not really know who Jesus is.

Meditation: Do you really know who Jesus is? Sketch a written portrait of him.

Prayer: God of Jesus, you have revealed yourself to us in the suffering, death, and resurrection of your Son. Through the gift of the Holy Spirit guide us in the ways of authentic discipleship and lead us to the kingdom, where you live in perfect Trinity: Father, Son and Holy Spirit, one God, for ever and ever. Amen.

NOT ACCEPTED

Luke 4:21-30

Scripture: "No prophet is accepted in his own hometown" (Luke 4:24).

Reflection: According to the Lucan narrative of events, Jesus begins his Galilean ministry by entering the synagogue in Nazareth on the Sabbath, reading from the scroll of the prophet Isaiah, preaching his first sermon, and being rejected by his own people. We are not dealing here with a series of historical details so much as we are with a theological narrative that has a refutable point — as far as Luke is concerned.

By having Jesus declare that "no prophet is accepted in his own hometown," Luke is forecasting what is going to happen immediately later in the same story and remotely later in the same work. Luke is fond of prophecy and fulfillment; that is, he tells the reader what is going to happen, and then later he shows it taking place. The author has plotted his narrative very carefully in this fashion.

Immediately following the declaration that "no prophet is accepted in his own hometown," Luke has Jesus remind his listeners (in the context of the section) and the reader (in the context of reading the Gospel) that neither Elijah nor Elisha were accepted by their own either.

The only great deeds that Elijah would be instrumental in

performing were done for a widow in Zarephath. Elisha could only direct the cure of Naaman the Syrian. In both cases, the deed done was not for an Israelite but for a pagan. In this way, Luke reminds the reader of the stubbornness and hardheartedness of his own people.

Luke is also declaring that Jesus is a prophet like Elijah and Elisha, that he will be rejected and able to work no great deeds for his own people, just as they were rejected and unable to perform great deeds for their own people. Therefore, this section of Luke's Gospel ends with the crowd driving Jesus out of the town; they are ready to kill him — a task they will accomplish later in the Gospel.

Meditation: Who are the prophets of today? In what ways do you reject them?

Prayer: God of Elijah and Elisha, when you were rejected by those whom you call your own, you made your dwelling with other people and worked your great deeds among them. Help us to recognize the prophets in our midst today. Open our ears to hear their message. Thus, may we witness your great deeds among us, as did the widow of Zarephath and Naaman the Syrian. We ask this through our Lord Jesus Christ, your Son, who lives and reigns with you and the Holy Spirit, one God, for ever and ever. Amen.

PIGS
Mark 5:1-20

Scripture: Jesus asked him, "What is your name?" and he said to him, "My name is legion, because there are many of us" (Mark 5:9).

Reflection: In Mark's Gospel, the healing of the Gerasene Demoniac is the longest account of an exorcism in the Gospel, as well as the most amusing.

The scene takes place in pagan territory, which is ruled by a Roman legion of soldiers. The man with the unclean spirits lives among the tombs — an important point to be noted in order to understand the significance of this account.

Like all other unclean spirits in Mark's Gospel, these know who Jesus is — "Son of the Most High God" (5:7). The reader will recall the "messianic secret" of the Gospel — unclean spirits know who Jesus is, but his own disciples are slow to figure it out.

In the pagan territory, there are swineherds with a herd of about 2000 swine — no small number! Again, the reader is alerted by the large number of swine in pagan territory and the fact that the most repulsive occupation to a Jew was that of a swineherd. Pigs were considered unclean and pork was never eaten by them.

The unclean spirits leave the man and enter into the swine, who rush to the sea and drown themselves. The unclean spirits called themselves "Legion," for they were many. Mark's humor is obvious — he is calling the Roman forces "pigs"!

The man is found "sitting" and "clothed" (5:15). He, who lived among the tombs, has been changed, converted. He wants to remain with Jesus as a disciple, but he is sent off to proclaim the good news to everyone.

An echo of this man's conversion and ensuing acceptance of discipleship is heard often in the Gospel of Mark and it always carries this message: discipleship is one's response to a death and resurrection (conversion) experience.

Meditation: When have you had a conversion experience? How did it lead you to discipleship?

Prayer: God of eternal life, you have never ceased to share yourself with your people. Enable us to discover you in the various experiences of our lives and to respond by following Jesus, your Son, who lives and reigns with you and the Holy Spirit, one God, for ever and ever. Amen.

AUTHENTIC BELIEVERS

Mark 5:21-43

Scripture: "Who touched my cloak?" "Little girl, I say to you, arise!" (Mark 5:30, 41)

Reflection: The account of the raising of the daughter of Jairus is divided into two parts with the healing of the unnamed woman with a hemorrhage sandwiched in between. This method of narration occurs in other parts of the Gospel, as it is one of Mark's literary styles.

In both stories the emphasis is placed on Jesus as healer. However, it is not what Jesus does that is most important. Rather, what is stressed is the faith of those who are healed.

The faith of Jairus is contrasted to the lack of faith of the crowd. The faith of the woman with the hemorrhage is contrasted to the lack of faith in Jesus' disciples. In both cases, Mark does not focus on the "power" of Jesus, but on the faith of authentic believers. So, the question, "Who touched me?" becomes an occasion for Marcan humor and an opportunity to point toward the woman's faith.

Likewise, it is not what Jesus does for Jairus' daughter, but the calling forth of his faith. The description of the little girl's awakening is a delightful example of Mark's attention to details.

Since the little girl is asleep, she will only need to be awakened. While the sleep metaphor is frequently used in reference to death, here Mark employs it to focus attention on the faith of

Jairus rather than on the "power" of Jesus to raise the dead. The child is called to arise from her sleep.

Jesus tells those with him to give the little girl "something to eat" (5:43). In chapter six the disciples will also be told to give the crowd of 5000 "something to eat" (6:37). Once again, the echo is built into the story by the craft of the writer.

The point being made by Mark centers on the process of conversion. A person dies to his or her old self and is raised to a new existence in which the food (Eucharist and fellow believers) of the community sustains one.

Meditation: In what ways does your parish community sustain your faith? In what ways do you contribute to this faith-sustaining process for others?

Prayer: God of life, you demonstrate your love for people by giving them eternal life. When we are weak, touch us with your healing hand. When we die, raise us to the new life which you share with Jesus, your Son, who lives and reigns with you and the Holy Spirit, one God, for ever and ever. Amen.

CARPENTER?

Mark 6:1-6

Scripture: "Isn't this the carpenter, the son of Mary...?"
(Mark 6:3)

Reflection: In the scene of the rejection of Jesus at Nazareth —
"his own hometown" (6:1) — Mark tackles a number of important issues and problems which were facing the community for
whom he wrote the Gospel. The main issue, around which the
others revolve, is the identity and consequent authority of Jesus.

First, it is on a Sabbath — a strict day of rest — that Jesus
and his disciples enter the synagogue. Mark portrays Jesus as a
teacher, who has no official authority to teach! So, the questions
of the crowd function as a cue for the reader. In Jewish mentality, for a person to be a great teacher, he had to study with another, older teacher, who passes on his wisdom to his student.
Jesus has no such background.

Second, Mark calls Jesus "the carpenter," a designation
given him by no other Gospel. He is also referred to by Mark in
this passage as "the son of Mary," which is unusual. In Judaism,
a son is normally identified by reference to his father. In essence,
Mark is dealing with Jesus' identity. He is raising the question
for the reader: Who is Jesus?

Again we come back to the fact that, in Mark, the unclean
spirits are able to identify who Jesus is — the "Son of the Most

High God" (5:7) — but Jesus' disciples and family do not know who he is. Now, in this scene, the townsfolk of Nazareth likewise fail to recognize him. They lack faith!

Mark wants the reader to identify Jesus for himself or herself. Just because a person is numbered among the disciples of Jesus, the family of Jesus, or the fellow townsfolk of Jesus does not imply that he or she believes. In fact, as the reader has already discovered and will discover again later in the Gospel, the authentic believer is found outside the obvious circle of believers. In Mark's Gospel, the obvious answer is not always the correct one.

Meditation: How do you answer this question: Who is Jesus?

Prayer: God of all believers, you sent Jesus to reveal to all people the wonders of your love. As a teacher, he revealed the mysteries of the kingdom. As your Son, he touched humankind with your healing hand. Make us authentic disciples so that you may work your mighty deeds among us. We ask this through Christ our Lord. Amen.

MISSIONARIES

Mark 6:7-13

Scripture: He (Jesus) summoned the Twelve and began to send them out two by two, and he gave them authority over unclean spirits... So they went off and proclaimed that the people should repent (Mark 6:7, 12).

Reflection: The mission of the Twelve, who are synonymous with the apostles in Mark's Gospel, is not a snippet of history from the days of Jesus, but, rather, it is a short account of what was going on at the time this Gospel was being written. It also functions as a justification for the missionary activity of the Church down through history.

The reader should notice that the Twelve are sent in pairs. What is at stake is credibility, since in Judaism there was a need for two witnesses to attest to the truth of a deed done.

The authority of the missioners comes from Jesus himself, as Mark narrates the scene. For those who questioned the missionary activity of the early Church, this passing on of teaching authority from master to students legitimates the spreading of the good news.

In Mark's community the way the mission was accomplished is also important. So, he details the way the missionary travels and dresses. Such distinctions make the missioner easily recognizable to others. Because they are able to bear authentic witness, because they share in Jesus' authority, and because they are easily recognized as missioners, the Twelve (and all missionaries) are able to do the things that Mark's Jesus does — drive out demons, anoint the sick with oil and cure them.

One other important Marcan theme emerges in this section of the Gospel — repentance. Repentance or conversion is a major theme of this Gospel. For Mark, repentance requires radical change, the re-orientation of one's life according to the pattern of Jesus — suffering, death, and resurrection. This message of repentance, inaugurated by Jesus himself at the opening of Mark's Gospel, is the most important message of the missionary.

Meditation: In what ways are you a missionary?

Prayer: God of missionaries, through the preaching and teaching of Jesus, your Son, you call all people to repentance and a change of heart. Through the guidance of your Spirit, move our hearts and send us out to proclaim the suffering, death, and resurrection of Jesus, who is Lord, for ever and ever. Amen.

JOHN THE BAPTIST
Mark 6:14-29

Scripture: People were saying, "John the Baptizer has been raised from the dead, and that is why these powers are at work in him." But others said, "He is Elijah" (Mark 6:14-15).

Reflection: At the time of the writing of Mark's Gospel, John the Baptist was not the problem he would later turn out to be for the early Church. Mark makes it clear that the role of the Baptizer is to prepare the way for the Lord — thus fulfilling the Isaian prophecy of a messenger-herald. Also, the Baptizer is a type of Elijah, who, in popular Jewish belief, was to return to the earth before the Messiah came.

In later years, this presentation of the Baptizer would cause a number of problems and spur Matthew to temper Mark's baptism scene of Jesus by John by inserting a short dialogue between the two in which Jesus acknowledges his superiority over John but wants John to perform the ritual anyway. If John baptized Jesus, then he must have been greater, some early Christians were concluding.

Luke chose the solution to this problem in another unique way. He places John in prison before he mentions Jesus' baptism. Therefore, the reader is never told who baptized Jesus — just that Jesus was baptized. In these ways the early Church solved some of its problems with John the Baptist.

Mark's account of the death of John at the request of Herodias' daughter, who had performed a dance which delighted Herod and his guests, is a miniature passion account. In other words, it functions as a prophecy of what is going to happen to Jesus.

In the story of the death of John, Herod not only fears him but acknowledges his righteousness and holiness. Later, it will be Pilate who plays the same role when he must condemn Jesus to death. Likewise, just as Herodias harbors a grudge against John and seeks a way to put him to death, so the leaders of the Jews campaign for Jesus' death.

Finally, after John's beheading — a martyrdom, a spilling of blood — some of his disciples take his body and lay it in a tomb. After Jesus' crucifixion — his martyrdom — some well-disposed persons (not his disciples) take down his body and place it in a tomb. In this masterful way, Mark has prepared the reader for the future scenes in his Gospel.

Meditation: Who are the John the Baptists today? How are you a John the Baptist?

Prayer: God of Elijah and John, in times past you sent your prophets to prepare the way when you were about to reveal yourself to your people. Today, raise up men and women who can recognize your presence and announce your mighty deeds to a waiting world. We ask this through our Lord Jesus Christ, your Son, who lives and reigns with you and the Holy Spirit, one God, for ever and ever. Amen.

DESERT

Mark 6:30-34

Scripture: "Come away privately, just yourselves, to a desert place and rest for a while" (Mark 6:31).

Reflection: In this section of his Gospel (6:30-34), Mark is using the image of the exodus to make a theological point. Previously (6:7-13), Jesus sent the Twelve on mission; now, they have returned and reported their success. If read carefully, the mission of the delegation organized by Joshua to reconnoiter the land of Canaan can be seen here.

It is no accident that in Mark's Gospel Jesus leads the apostles to a desert place. It was in the desert, after the escape from Egyptian slavery, that God formed his people through the Law. Jesus, likewise, gathers his followers and teaches them his way in a desert place.

God worked through Moses; that is, God gave Moses special abilities to mold and hold together the Israelites. In fact, Moses (and his successors) was so attractive as a leader that other peoples (usually called foreigners) actively sought to join the Israelites. Mark uses this background in his portrayal of the "vast crowd," who follow Jesus.

In the next scene of the Gospel, Mark tells the first of two feeding stories, which echo the manna in the desert. While the early Christian eucharistic overtones are obvious, Mark's emphasis is on the teaching, the word of Jesus, which precedes the multiplication of loaves and fishes.

With this understanding, it is not difficult to see why Christianity has always had a fondness for the desert. Monasticism had its beginnings in the wasteland. Countless saints have spent untold years in the desert. Today, every person is encouraged to go away for a while and rest in a deserted or semi-deserted place, both for a short period each day for prayer and at least once a year for a retreat or other type of spiritual formation and evaluation.

In the desert there are no distractions. A person cannot be preoccupied by a hundred other things. There, in the desert, God can speak to the heart and mold it according to his way.

Meditation: In what ways do you satisfy your need for a daily (and yearly) desert experience?

Prayer: God of the desert, through Moses you led your people out of Egypt into the desert, where you nourished them with your Law and formed them into your own people. Through Jesus you lead us out of our preoccupations with the things of this world into the silence of your presence, where you nourish us with your word. Form us into a people who are eager to do your will. We ask this through your Son, our Lord Jesus Christ, who lives and reigns with you and the Holy Spirit in perfect Trinity, one God, for ever and ever. Amen.

SALT AND LIGHT
Matthew 5:13-16

Scripture: "You are the salt of the earth. You are the light of the world" (Matthew 5:13, 14).

Reflection: The metaphor of salt and the one concerning light, which follows it, form the second part of Jesus' first sermon in the Gospel of Matthew; the first part of the sermon consists of the nine beatitudes.

After naming blessed, that is possessing characteristics of God, those who were not considered blessed in the mindset of the time, Jesus metaphorically explains how these blessed function in the world — like salt and like light.

There are two ways to understand the salt analogy. In the first instance, the blessed are seasoning for the world, just as salt brings out the flavor of food. Once applied, the salt cannot be removed from food. Similarly, the blessed followers of Jesus are in the world flavoring it with the ways of Jesus. Salt also preserves. If the blessed fail, they are like salt that has lost its saltiness or its ability to bring out flavor and to preserve; they are useless.

Secondly, the "earth" in the phrase "salt of the earth" could refer to the large outdoor earthen ovens, which were used to bake bread. Since wood was scarce, the ovens were fueled with camel dung. Salt, mixed with the dung, functioned as a catalyst; it enabled the fire to burn steadily and hotter. Therefore, the blessed are catalysts for authentic discipleship. Later in the Gospel of Matthew, Jesus will echo this theme when he speaks of setting a fire on the earth.

The second metaphor of light is suffused with humor. The typical fat, tallow, or oil lamp gave less light than candles, which were expensive to own. So, a tiny flickering lamp was set on a stand so that as many people as possible could benefit from its light. To light it and put it under a bushel basket was silly to the point of being ridiculous.

The good deeds of the blessed are like a tiny lamp. They witness the way of Jesus and glorify the Father. When many such lights are grouped together, as in a city set on a mountain, the light of good deeds cannot be hidden from others, who are, hopefully, influenced to add their light and salt to the community.

Meditation: In what ways are you salt and light?

Prayer: God of salt and light, from the beginning of time you have flavored the earth with your presence. In these last days, you have spread your light in Jesus, your Son. Enable our good deeds to witness to the power of your love, which is eternally shared with Jesus and the Holy Spirit, one God, for ever and ever. Amen.

PREACHING AND TEACHING

Mark 1:29-39

Scripture: "Let's go elsewhere, to the neighboring country towns, so I can preach there as well — this is what I came for" (Mark 1:38)

Reflection: In twenty-four verses (1:21-45) of the first chapter of his Gospel, Mark portrays one day in the life of Jesus. In this section are found exorcisms, healings, and teaching which take place throughout the day and into the evening and the following morning.

Two Marcan characteristics of Jesus emerge from this picture. First, most of these deeds are done on the Sabbath, which was regulated by a whole collection of laws. By performing such mighty works on the Sabbath, Jesus was violating these laws and exerting his own authority.

Secondly, although he is clearly portrayed as a teacher/ preacher, the content of Jesus' teaching is never central to Mark. His emphasis is placed, rather, on the announcement of the kingdom of God being at hand and the repentance which should flow forth from this good news.

In effect, in Mark, Jesus always seems to be in a hurry. He travels quickly from one place to another and does more in one day than most people are able to do in a week!

This unique presentation of Jesus by Mark gives the whole

story an urgency and pushes the reader on to the next section of the Gospel in order to see where Jesus is headed next and what he will be doing there.

His purpose in all of this traveling is to preach. As Mark portrays Jesus' audience, his preaching had effect; that is, those who believed experienced the kingdom of God in Jesus. The reader, likewise, can experience it by reading and believing in the Gospel.

Meditation: Today, who are the preachers who proclaim the kingdom of God and move you to repentance and a deeper faith in the Gospel?

Prayer: God of good news, in every time and place you have sent men and women who have orally proclaimed your mighty deeds. Through the written word of the Scriptures you continue to make yourself known. Send us preachers who are on fire with the message of the Gospel, that we might be moved to repentance and a deeper faith. We ask this through our Lord Jesus Christ, your Son, who lives and reigns with you and the Holy Spirit, one God, for ever and ever. Amen.

CATCHING PEOPLE
Luke 5:1-11

Scripture: Jesus said to Simon, "Don't be afraid; from now on you'll be catching men" (Luke 5:10).

Reflection: The call of the fishermen, Simon (Peter), James, and John, is found in all of the synoptics (Matthew, Mark, Luke). Yet, the placement of the scene and the way each evangelist portrays it reveals a different emphasis and theological perspective.

In Matthew and Mark, the fishing metaphor refers to the future fate of the disciples. Like a fish that is caught and dies, once one has been hooked by Jesus his or her fate may be like that of Jesus — death!

Luke uses the incident in two ways. First, by placing an emphasis on Simon (Peter) he contrasts Simon's acceptance of Jesus to the hometown denial of Jesus. Here, Simon occupies center stage in contrast to Mark and Matthew, who present an equal call to Simon and Andrew, who is not mentioned here, and James and John.

Second, Luke is anticipating the ensuing success of Simon's ministry in the Acts of the Apostles (volume two of Luke's two-volume work). As a future leader, Simon will catch people.

Another interest note in this narrative is Simon's address to Jesus as "Lord." The post-resurrection title of "Lord" has been read back into the text. In this way, Luke, using his favorite prophecy-fulfillment literary technique, gives the reader a hint of the end of the Gospel and the future success of the Church, which designated Jesus as its "Lord."

Furthermore, the portrayal of Simon's obedience to Jesus' command to lower the nets after a night of futility, represents the willingness of the Church to submit herself to her Lord, while at the same time being conscious of her sinful state and her need for him.

Meditation: In what ways has the Lord called you to discipleship? In other words, how have you been hooked?

Prayer: God of fishermen, you send your word as bait to your people, and you raise up men and women who preach your good news. Give success to all their fishing endeavors. Move our hearts to be hooked on every syllable of the Gospel of your Son, Jesus Christ, who lives and reigns with you and the Holy Spirit, one God for ever and ever. Amen.

POWERLESS HEALING

Mark 6:53-56

Scripture: Wherever he entered the villages or cities or farms, they put the sick in the marketplaces and begged him to let them just touch the tassel of his cloak; and all who touched it were saved (Mark 6:56).

Reflection: In this last verse of chapter six of Mark's Gospel, the author presents Jesus as a healer once again. No specific person is mentioned; rather, Jesus heals all the sick from the villages, towns and surrounding countryside. In the community for whom Mark wrote this Gospel, Jesus was definitely remembered as an itinerant healer.

But the Marcan style comes through nevertheless. Those sick who were able to touch the tassel of Jesus' cloak were healed. This Marcan touch is an echo of an earlier healing of the woman with the hemorrhage in chapter five who was able to touch Jesus' clothes and immediately experience healing.

In narrating these healings, what is Mark's interest? For the reader, these healings can leave the impression of a powerful Messiah, who, when his cloak is touched, generates healing for those who need it. This type of hero, from a literary perspective, is very appealing. The reader is easily edified by such a character and will read on to see what more he or she will accomplish.

And this is exactly what Mark has done. He wins the reader over in the first eight chapters of the Gospel with his portrayal of a healing, miracle-working, exorcising Messiah. However, in chapter eight, the reader will suddenly find his expectations turned up-side down — converted, as it were — as he or she learns that Messiahship requires suffering, death, and resurrection. It is in powerlessness that real power resides.

What Mark has done is to use the tradition of Jesus as a healer of physical ills to push the meaning of healing in a new direction. Mark is not interested in physical healings; he is interested in making the reader realize that physical healings are not sufficient reason to believe in Jesus. He downplays the power of Jesus, a power to which every person is attracted. In power's place, Mark has set powerlessness. A person believes in Jesus, not because of Jesus' ability to heal, but because one has come to see that real power consists in powerlessness.

Meditation: In what recent experience have you experienced powerlessness as power?

Prayer: God of power, you always care for your people. Through Jesus, your servant and your Son, you brought your healing touch to humankind. As we continue our pilgrimage to you, strengthen our faith in the powerlessness of the suffering, death, and resurrection of Jesus, who lives and reigns with you and the Holy Spirit, one God, for ever and ever. Amen.

TRADITION
Mark 7:1-13

Scripture: "Why don't your disciples follow the tradition of the elders but instead eat bread with unclean hands?" (Mark 7:5)

Reflection: The beginning of chapter seven of Mark's Gospel presents another conflict situation between Jesus and the scribes and Pharisees. The conflict is mirrored in the conflict of the early Church between the Jewish Christians and the Gentile converts of Mark's community.

Mark sets the stage by posing the tradition of the elders, that is, the custom of washing hands, food, cups, kettles, etc. To many Jews, this body of detailed written and unwritten human law was regarded as having the same binding force as the Torah, the law of Moses. Therefore, it was only natural that some Jewish Christians would feel that the Gentiles who wished to follow Jesus would have to adopt this body of law as well.

What Mark is declaring here is that this is not the case. Conversion is not based on adopting Jewish laws or Jewish purification rituals. Authentic conversion to discipleship involves the heart of each person. It is easy to keep the law; in fact keeping the law can become mere lip service. But once the heart has been converted, then keeping the law is no longer the question. Once authentic conversion has taken place, a person will go beyond the law.

The case exists today of the person who dutifully attends the celebration of the Eucharist (commonly referred to as "going to Mass") every Sunday. However, the motivation for doing so is the obligation imposed on every Catholic by Church law.

Contrast this person to the one who also celebrates the Eucharist every Sunday but does so out of desire to join the Christian community — to hear the word and eat and drink at the Lord's table.

Both Christians are keeping the law. Which of the two, however, has moved beyond the law? It is obvious that the second has. Authentic conversion is not about keeping the law nor is it about paying mere lip service; authentic conversion is about a change which takes place in an individual's heart.

Meditation: Why do you keep the law?

Prayer: God of the law, once you led your people from slavery to freedom, and through Moses you gave them your law in order to train their hearts according to your ways. In the fullness of time you gave us your eternal Word, Jesus, who taught us your law of love and called us to authentic discipleship. Through the power of your Holy Spirit, move our hearts to authentic conversion. We ask this through Christ our Lord. Amen.

MORAL CONVERSION

Mark 7:14-23

Scripture: "Don't you see that nothing that enters a person from outside can make one unclean? ... What comes out of a person, that is what makes him unclean" (Mark 7:19-20).

Reflection: This section of Mark's Gospel continues the discussion, which was begun in yesterday's passage about clean and unclean foods. Here in Mark Jesus is carefully abrogating the Mosaic food laws and pushing the question of ritual washing to a different level.

In the kingdom of God, ritual washings are not important, Mark is saying. In order to be sure that the reader gets the point, the author himself enters into the text parenthetically when he writes, "Thus he (Jesus) declared all foods to be clean" (7:19). This point is made for two reasons.

First, by declaring all foods clean, the door is opened to the Gentiles. Mark is attempting to show that Gentiles can enter the kingdom of God. For this reason, in the next scene of this Gospel, Mark places Jesus in the district of Tyre from which he then travels by way of Sidon to the Sea of Galilee into the district of the Decapolis — all of them Gentile territories. Thus, by portraying a ministry of Jesus to the Gentiles, Mark states theologically that Jesus has made it possible for all people to share in the kingdom of God.

Second, the declaration that all foods are clean was evidently not definitively settled by Jesus for in the early Church the Jewish purification rituals and the distinction between clean and unclean foods continued to be a real problem. This is reflected in the Acts of the Apostles (10:1-11:18) where we find some in the early Church arguing that Gentiles would have to adopt all Jewish practices before they could be declared Christians. Through the leadership of Paul, the first ecumenical council of the Church in Jerusalem decreed differently.

Having cleared up this problem with his usual literary flair, Mark makes another important point, which is echoed earlier in the Gospel. This is the hidden quality of the meaning of parables. In 4:10-11, 34, the author states that Jesus spoke in parables to the crowd but revealed their meaning to the disciples.

Mark builds on this point in this section when he portrays Jesus leaving the crowd with his disciples in order to explain the parable to them privately. "Nothing that enters a person from outside can make one unclean.... What comes out of a person, that is what makes him unclean" (Mark 7:15). The explanation pushes the question of the Mosaic food laws beyond ritual washings and sprinklings to the moral plane.

The real question as Mark sees it is a moral one. Authentic conversion to discipleship involves a moral turning around — a leaving behind of what comes from within the heart: evil thoughts, fornication, theft, murder, adultery, greed, evil intentions, deceit, indecency, jealousy, blasphemy, arrogance, and folly (cf. 7:21-22). To be declared a follower of Jesus has nothing to do with the observance of ritual washings and sprinklings and clean and unclean foods; rather an authentic follower of Jesus is morally converted in his or her heart. This is the point of the first twenty-three verses of chapter seven of Mark's Gospel.

Meditation: Recently, in what ways have you been morally converted in your heart?

Prayer: God of conversion, you never cease to call your people to turn back to you. Through covenants you bound yourself to your people, if they would follow your ways. In Jesus, your servant and your Son, you established a new covenant. Through the power of your Holy Spirit, move our hearts to authentic conversion so that we might be numbered among the disciples of Jesus, who is Lord for ever and ever. Amen.

DOGS
Mark 7:24-30

Scripture: "Lord, even the pups beneath the table eat the children's crumbs" (Mark 7:28).

Reflection: The above quotation is spoken by a Greek woman, who was Syrophoenician by birth. She had a daughter who "had an unclean spirit" (7:25) and "she kept begging Jesus to drive the demon out of her daughter" (7:26).

The story consists of a simple dialogue between the woman and Jesus. However, in his typical theologically-laden storytelling style, Mark has crafted a narrative which addresses a number of problems of his own community.

First, Mark portrays Jesus as traveling to the district of Tyre. This is Gentile territory. Furthermore, the woman who approaches Jesus is clearly indicated to be a Gentile — a Greek, a Syrophoenician by birth.

Mark portrays Jesus as a typical Jew. His comment, "Let the children be fed first. It isn't right to take the children's bread and throw it to the pups" (7:27), is metaphorical. In a household, after the children were fed, the leftover scraps were given to the household dogs, who usually rested and waited under the table.

Here, Jesus metaphorically refers to the Jews as children and to the Gentiles as pups. In effect, he seems to be calling the woman's daughter a dog. This, of course, is not the picture of Jesus that most Christians treasure, nor is it the one Mark wants to leave us with. This image is used only to make a theological point.

That point is made by the woman, "Lord, even the pups beneath the table eat the children's crumbs" (7:28). In other words, the woman is declaring that Gentiles should be able to benefit from the ministry of Jesus. How craftily Mark has justified the mission to the Gentiles!

Second, the mission to the Gentiles is based on faith. Because the woman believed and stood up to Jesus, her daughter was cured. Again, Mark is making an important point: faith, no matter whether one is a Jew or a Gentile, is what characterizes an authentic disciple of Jesus.

Third, it is important to note that it is a woman who gets the best of Jesus. In this Gospel, Mark is particularly sensitive to women and their needs. They occupy key positions throughout the Gospel. Why? Because in general, they were powerless people. What Mark is attempting to show is that it is the powerless who are really powerful. This theme is developed more in the second half of the Gospel.

Meditation: From your own experience, what separates Christians today? What unites Christians today?

Prayer: God of all people, you created man and woman in your own image and likeness and you called them to walk always with you. Guide us in tearing down the walls that divide. Help us to eliminate all prejudice. Enable us to love one another, so that we may share in the unity of your Son and your Holy Spirit, who live and reign with you, one God, for ever and ever. Amen

BE OPENED!
Mark 7:31-37

Scripture: The people there brought him a deaf and tongue-tied man and begged him to lay his hands on him. He... put his finger into his ears and, after spitting, he touched his tongue. Then he looked up to heaven, sighed, and said to him, "Ephphatha!" (Mark 7:32-34)

Reflection: In this account of the healing of the deaf man with the speech impediment, Mark has skillfully taken a healing story and woven a tapestry out of it. In order to understand the theological point of the story, the reader must consider a number of things.

First, this healing takes place in Gentile territory. The man, it is presumed, is a Gentile. By portraying Jesus as healing a Gentile, Mark is continuing his justification for the early Church's mission to the Gentiles. As has been previously stated, all of chapter seven wrestles with the question of the extension of Jesus' Jewish ministry to those outside of Judaism.

Second, the place of this account of the deaf man with a speech impediment is no accident in the context of the whole of the Gospel. In Mark Jesus has been teaching the crowds and his disciples, who never seem to understand what he is telling them. Now, Mark presents a deaf man — one who cannot hear, but who does understand — in contrast to those who can hear and do not understand. Furthermore, the deaf man is a Gentile.

The theological statement comes through loud and clear: a

person, no matter whether he or she is Jewish or Gentile, is capable of hearing the word of God and responding positively to it.

Third, it is important to note that Jesus takes the man off by himself, away from the crowd before the healing takes place. For Mark, conversion and faith are personal matters between the individual and Jesus.

Fourth, the response of the crowd, which finds out about the healing, is to "proclaim" this deed. The verb used here is the same used in other places to indicate the preaching of the Gospel, the good news, by Jesus, his disciples, and, of course, the early Christian community. Put simply, once one has been converted and comes to faith, one cannot help but proclaim it to others. Therefore, the deaf man's speech impediment has also been healed.

Fifth, this story immediately precedes the account of the feeding of the four thousand, after which there is a demand for a sign and a great misunderstanding by Jesus' disciples. The reader's own conversion and faith is, thus, challenged at this point. He or she must ask if he or she is an authentic believer or just a member of the crowd, who seem to believe at one instance and then change their minds at the next.

Sixth, the healing of the deaf and mute man echoes the statement of Jesus found in chapter four of Mark's Gospel: "To you is given the secret of the kingdom of God, but to those outside everything is given in parables, so that 'although they look, they may see yet not perceive, and though they listen, they may hear yet not understand, lest they be converted and find forgiveness.'" (4:11-12). This man has heard and listened and been converted. Now he shares in the mystery of the kingdom of God.

Meditation: In what ways have you recently heard the word of God, been converted, and proclaimed this good news to others?

Prayer: God of those who cannot hear, you speak your word of truth to your people and you open their ears that they might hear. You touch their tongues that they might proclaim the mighty deeds of Jesus, your Son. Open our ears and loosen our tongues that we might make you known throughout all the world. We ask this through Christ our Lord. Amen.

PITY

Mark 8:1-10

Scripture: "I'm overcome with pity for the crowd, because they've stayed with me for three days now and don't have anything to eat" (Mark 8:2).

Reflection: The narrative of the feeding of the four thousand is very similar to the narrative of the feeding of the five thousand in chapter six. In fact, most Scripture scholars contend that only one original story is behind both narratives. From one story there grew two distinct traditions, and Mark recorded both of them.

The narrative of the feeding of the four thousand is not interested in some historical incident (although there may be such an incident behind it), but Mark is interested in teasing a eucharistic significance out of the story.

The use of the sacred numbers three and seven indicate a theophany, a manifestation of God. Three three-year-old animals are slaughtered when Abraham enters into a covenant with God. Sarah prepares three seahs of fine flour, when three unexpected visitors deliver a message that she will give birth to Isaac.

Seven indicates totality or fullness or completeness. Six days of creation are followed by the seventh day of rest. Naaman washes seven times in the Jordan and is healed of his leprosy.

What Mark is declaring is that the Christian Eucharist represents the fullness of the manifestation of God. Those people who share in the loaves are not only satisfied, but seven baskets remain.

This complete manifestation of God is Mark's emphasis, rather than a focus on an event of the multiplication of loaves and fishes. The concern of the crowd, who are hungry for the word of God, is the point of the story. People can have their hunger satisfied by Jesus, in his word and in the Eucharist.

Meditation: In the past three days, in what seven ways has God revealed himself to you?

Prayer: God of the loaves and fishes, in the desert you fed your people with manna and quail. Through Moses you satisfied their hunger with your law. In the fullness of time, Jesus, your Son, fed people with your word and manifested in human flesh the wonders of your love. Give us the bread of life and teach us the wisdom of your law so that one day we may be satisfied and live with you, your Son, and your Holy Spirit, one God, for ever and ever. Amen.

RIGHTEOUSNESS

Matthew 5:17-37

Scripture: "I tell you, unless your righteousness greatly exceeds that of the scribes and Pharisees, you'll never get into the kingdom of heaven" (Matthew 5:20).

Reflection: The first chapter of Matthew's Gospel, as well as the first great sermon of Jesus in chapters five through seven, deals with the issue of righteousness. For Matthew, righteousness is another word for holiness. It is that quality of God which sets things right; it is the way one is supposed to be.

In Matthew's first chapter, Joseph is held up as the righteous individual. However, he is righteous not because he does not follow the law and put Mary away quietly, but because he breaks the law by taking her as his wife. Thus, Joseph becomes the paradigm of the righteous person. Joseph's righteousness exceeds the keeping of the law.

In Jesus' first of five great sermons, Matthew further explores this understanding of righteousness. He believes that the law (Torah) and the prophets will continue to have their importance, but what needs to be worked on is the doing or the keeping of the commandments. So, he is not interested in abolishing the law, but he is interested in exploring how people not only succeed but exceed the keeping of the law.

The standard, as Matthew understands it, for teaching and doing is righteousness. A person obeys the law not for the sake of obedience, but for the sake of authenticity, which is a higher or greater form of righteousness. In this re-interpretation of the law, what is authentic cannot be stated in words but in the intention of the "doer."

If the law declares that one should not kill another, then righteousness demands that one does not even get angry with another. Anything that separates one person from another in the kingdom of heaven is murder. If a person is not reconciled with others then that person is also not reconciled with God.

If the law declares that women are objects of shame and are of lesser worth than men, then the righteous person goes beyond the law and declares that men and women are equal. Women are elevated to a position of honor by Matthew; they are of equal status with men. Therefore, they can be offended. The issue is not adultery per se; the issue is the equality of women.

If the law insists that one call on God to witness a deed in an oath, Jesus declares in Matthew's Gospel that God cannot guarantee a relationship between two people; only the honesty of the two individuals involved in the relationship can guarantee it. The righteous person is able to stand on his or her own truthfulness; there is no need to swear. All one has to do is say "Yes" when yes is meant and to say "No" when no is meant. This is enough.

The way of righteousness, as Jesus presents it, is not easy. It is much easier to keep the law than it is to rise above it. Sometimes, people have to break the law (as Joseph did) in order to be truly righteous.

Meditation: In what ways are you righteous (especially in the areas of anger, women, and honesty)?

Prayer: God of righteousness, through Moses you gave your people the law, and through the prophets you continued to teach them how to obey and keep it. Through Jesus, you fulfilled the law and taught us a righteousness that even exceeds it. Give us your Holy Spirit to help us follow and practice your ways. We ask this through Christ our Lord. Amen.

RE-UNITED

Mark 1:40-45

Scripture: A leper came up to Jesus (and kneeling down) begged him, saying to him, "If you wish to, you can make me clean!" Greatly moved, he reached out his hand, touched him, and said to him, "I do will it. Be made clean" (Mark 1:40-41).

Reflection: In the modern world, the disease of leprosy is seldom heard of anymore. For the most part, it has almost been eradicated from the face of the earth.

However, at the time of the writing of Mark's Gospel (around 70 A.D.), leprosy was still a contagious disease. The person who contracted the disease not only had to contend with the illness, but he or she was ostracized from the rest of society.

Although there are many types of leprosy, the basic form consisted of an open cancerous sore. By law the leper had to stay out of public places; if he or she came near other people, he or she had to announce his or her presence by crying out, "Unclean! Unclean!"

The narrative of the incident of Jesus and the leper not only carries with it a theological point, but it portrays Jesus as one who heals by touch. The first readers of this passage would have cringed with disbelief, because one did not touch a leper — as Jesus did. To do so was to place oneself in jeopardy of getting the disease.

Mark's Jesus is one of compassion, however. He is moved with pity for the leper. So, he stretches out his hand and touches him. An echo from the Old Testament is heard here. The mighty hand of God is extended and mighty deeds result. In the person of Jesus of Nazareth, Mark is declaring, God has visited his people.

Another of Mark's theological points deals with the importance of inclusion in society. Because leprosy separated people, Mark emphasizes that Jesus' healing re-unites people. So the man is told to show himself to the priest, who was responsible for re-instating cured lepers to the community. Mark is declaring that people segregate themselves; Jesus brought people together.

A third important point to note in this healing story is the fact that the man proclaims the mighty deeds of God in his life. Because of his experience of healing, he declares what God has done for him. In effect, Mark is saying that this man has become a disciple. He is contrasted, of course, to the "official" disciples, who never recognize Jesus throughout Mark's Gospel.

Today, the disease that is in need of healing, the disease that separates people is AIDS. AIDS has become the new leprosy. Mark's Jesus reminds his readers that such a patient needs compassion, understanding, and acceptance. The worst thing that can happen is ostracization.

The person with leprosy (read AIDS), Mark cautions, may be an authentic disciple of Jesus. He or she may be proclaiming the mighty deeds of God in his or her life. However, if ostracized by others, these others may never hear this good news.

Meditation: What is your attitude toward people with AIDS, cancer, other terminal diseases?

Prayer: God of healing, the hand of your loving care reaches from east to west and from north to south. When your people suffer, you give them the strength to praise your name. Teach us the value of suffering, and enable us to reach out with compassion and touch those in need of your healing power. We ask this through our Lord Jesus Christ, your Son, who lives and reigns with you and the Holy Spirit, one God for ever and ever. Amen.

ON THE PLAIN

Luke 6:17, 20-26

Scripture: When (Jesus) came down (from the mountain) with them (the Twelve), he stood on a stretch of level ground and a large crowd of his disciples as well as a great number of the people… came to hear him (Luke 6:17-18).

Reflection: This particular section of Luke's Gospel is comparable to Matthew's first great sermon of Jesus on a mountain. Matthew, writing for a Jewish-Christian audience, portrays Jesus delivering his sermon on a mountain because Matthew understands Jesus to be a new Moses, who goes to the mountain and delivers five sermons (parallel to the five books of the Law — Genesis, Exodus, Leviticus, Numbers and Deuteronomy).

Luke, however, writing for an upper class Gentile society, cannot portray Jesus as a new Moses because this would make no sense to his audience. So, he sets the scene for the teaching of the beatitudes on a "stretch of level ground"; hence, the sermon is usually referred to as the sermon on the plain.

In contrast to the nine Matthean beatitudes, Luke records only four beatitudes with four corresponding "woes."

This peculiar Lucan set, of course, emphasizes Luke's major Gospel themes which had to do with the economic and social conditions of people at the time that his Gospel was written: the poor vs. the rich; the hungry vs. the satisfied; those grieving vs. those laughing; the outcast vs. the socially acceptable.

First, for Luke the poor are those who are economically deprived, those who are at the bottom rung of the ladder. Throughout his Gospel these are contrasted with the rich, Luke's audience. Luke cautions his readers to be careful to take care of the needs of the poor, to use their riches to assist those who have no material resources. For Luke, the kingdom of God belongs to the poor: "... the poor are given the good news" (7:22). The rich, with whom Luke has a lot of problems, will find it difficult to enter the kingdom of God (cf. 18:18-30).

Second, closely aligned with the poor are those who are hungry. Feeding the hungry is another major thrust of Luke's Gospel. It appears as early as the Canticle of Mary ("... the hungry he has filled with good things," 1:53) and continues through the feeding of the five thousand (9:12-17), the parable of the great feast (14:15-24), and the appearance on the road to Emmaus (24:13-35). Both the theme of the poor and the hungry are tied together by Luke in the parable of the rich man and Lazarus (16:19-31).

Third, the weeping, who will one day laugh, are scattered throughout the Gospel in stories such as the healing of the centurion's slave, the raising of the widow's son (7:1-17), and Jairus' daughter and the woman with a hemorrhage (8:40-56).

Fourth, the last beatitude is addressed to the early Christians who were hated, excluded, insulted and denounced. For Luke, these are signs of authentic discipleship; this is the cost of discipleship (cf. 9:23-27). This is also Luke's way of letting the reader know what will happen to Jesus, the Son of Man: he will be hated, excluded, insulted, denounced, and put to death. Persons who profess to be disciples must be willing to endure the same.

Meditation: In what ways are you poor, hungry, weeping, hated, excluded, insulted, and denounced on account of the Son of Man? In what ways are you rich, filled, laughing, and spoken well of?

Prayer: God of the poor, the hungry, the weeping, and the hated, you give your kingdom to the poor; you feed the hungry with every good thing; you bring laughter to the weeping; and you raise to new life those who are hated on account of the Son of Man, Jesus. Form in us the ways of authentic discipleship that we might bring to all we meet the good news of your kingdom, where you live with your Son and the Holy Spirit, one God, for ever and ever. Amen.

NO SIGNS
Mark 8:11-13

Scripture: "Why does this generation seek a sign? Amen, I say to you, no sign will be given to this generation" (Mark 8:12).

Reflection: Mark's Gospel was written for any person who thinks that faith consists of belief in signs. This is a presupposition that undergirds the whole Gospel.

The first part of the Gospel presents a Jesus who has power to heal, to exorcise, and to work miracles. However, in the middle of chapter eight this is all set aside by the author who will insist that a person should accept Jesus as the Messiah not because he could heal, exorcise or work miracles — all demonstrations of power — but because he suffered, died, and was raised from the dead.

For Mark, authentic faith in Jesus is not based on signs. He places the short narrative of the Pharisees' demand for a sign immediately after the narrative of the healing of the deaf man and the feeding of the four thousand. It would be easy for the reader to conclude that these signs (healing, multiplication of loaves and fishes) are sufficient reasons to belive in Jesus. For Mark, however, miracles or signs do not prove anything. For Mark, a person believes in Jesus because Jesus is like them — powerlessly human! This theme is fully developed from the middle of chapter eight to the end of the Gospel.

In refusing to give the reader any sign, Mark is being faithful to the first commandment — God has no image; he is not an idol. To make anyone an idol or a sign is to fall into the temptation of idolatry. Mark does not want to turn Jesus into an idol. He portrays Jesus as one who exactly resembles God who cannot be imaged. So the author presents a powerful Jesus, who heralds the kingdom of God in the first half of the Gospel. Then, he presents a human, powerless Jesus, who suffers, dies and is raised in the second half of the Gospel. In this way he proclaims the good news through Jesus, but he refuses to create an idol of him or to make of him a sign.

For Mark, Jesus is like God in the sense that the most that anyone can say about God is nothing, and when nothing has been said, all that can be said has been spoken! Therefore, once a lot has been said about Jesus, the author must conclude that whatever has been said must be unsaid (nothing), otherwise, he would have created an idol, a sign.

This lack-of-a-sign theme reaches a crescendo in the last chapter (16) and the original ending (16:1-8) of the Gospel. First, there is no post-resurrection appearance of Jesus. Second, there are no witnesses to the resurrection. Third, the women leave the tomb and say nothing to anyone.

What these three points add up to is this: there can be no signs. A person either believes or he or she does not believe. The furthering of this Gospel message is left to the reader who is cautioned to put no stock in signs.

Meditation: Why do you believe?

Prayer: God without an image, you revealed your power in the human powerlessness of Jesus of Nazareth. Open our hearts to the words of the good news, which he proclaimed, and strengthen our faith in him, who lives and reigns with you and the Holy Spirit, one God, for ever and ever. Amen.

UNDERSTAND?

Mark 8:14-21

Scripture: "Do you still not see or understand? Do you have hardened hearts? Can't you see with your eyes? Can't you hear with your ears?" (Mark 8:17)

Reflection: In the warning that Jesus gives to the disciples about the leaven of the Pharisees, Mark is two steps from winding down the first half of his story, inverting it, and beginning part two. The discussion with Jesus in this passage reveals a number of points which Mark has been offering the reader for consideration.

First, in his typical literary flair, Mark recalls the feeding of the five thousand and the feeding of the four thousand by stating that the disciples "had forgotten to bring bread, and except for one loaf they had none with them in the boat" (8:14). Mark is cuing the reader to remember what happened with only a few loaves, when so many were hungry!

Second, just as the first account of the feeding of the five thousand is followed by a scene with Jesus and the disciples in a boat, so is the second account of the feeding of the four thousand followed by a similar scene. The Marcan parallels are too obvious to miss.

Mark is making this statement through the use of these two literary techniques: the crowds had their hunger satisfied. The disciples witnessed this, but they did not understand. Therefore, they have no bread.

Even later in this same section they are characterized as still not understanding. Jesus questions them: "'When I broke the five loaves for the five thousand, how many baskets full of leftovers did you pick up?' 'Twelve,' they said. 'And when I broke the seven loaves for the four thousand, how many full baskets of leftovers did you pick up?' 'Seven,' they said" (8:19-20).

The disciples should have understood. Twelve signifies the tribes of Israel, a people chosen by God. Seven indicates fullness or completion. Mark is telling the reader to not miss this significance. Jesus has chosen a new group of Twelve. Jesus is the fullness of the kingdom of God.

Third, the warning Jesus issues to the disciples is about the "leaven of the Pharisees and the leaven of Herod." Leaven, which was used in making bread — much like yeast is used today — was employed as a substance to cause fermentation in the dough. Just as leaven is used to make bread — bread which Jesus used to feed thousands and thus, to cause fermentation in their lives as they sought to pursue the ways of the kingdom — so are the ways of the Pharisees and Herod going to bring ferment into the life of Jesus. Mark is hinting about what is going to happen to Jesus later in the Gospel: his life will be corrupted by the leaven of the Pharisees and Herod; that is, he will be put to death.

Fourth, when Jesus asks the disciples, "Do you have hardened hearts?" (8:17), he is posing an explosive question to them. The Israelites were constantly warned by the prophets about allowing their hearts to become hardened because they were forever turning away from worship of the one true God. To ask/accuse the disciples of hardened hearts is one of the worst things Jesus could have said.

However, this portrayal of the disciples is in keeping with Mark's theme of the misunderstanding Twelve. He is, of course, questioning the reader: "Do *you* still not understand?" (8:21). This is equivalent to asking, "Do you still not believe?"

Meditation: How have you been leavened by the words of Jesus?

Prayer: God of bread, when your people were hungry in the desert, you sent them manna. When your people were hungry for your word, you sent them Jesus, your Son. He preached and taught about your kingdom and thus brought ferment into the lives of all who would listen and understand him. Give us our daily bread and leaven us with your good news. We ask this through Christ our Lord. Amen.

BLIND

Mark 8:22-26

Scripture: Once again (Jesus) laid his hands on the man's eyes; then his sight was restored and he could see everything clearly (Mark 8:25).

Reflection: The account of the healing of the blind man of Bethsaida (8:22-26) and the narrative of the healing of the blind Bartimaeus (10:46-52) function as a frame for the core of Mark's Gospel. From chapter eight, verse 27, to the end of chapter 10, through theological images, Mark lays out his understanding of conversion and discipleship. In these verses, he also displays the whole tapestry, whose threads he has been revealing and weaving throughout the first part of the Gospel.

It is no accident that the story of a blind man precedes Peter's confession about Jesus. The details of the story reveal the theological point Mark is attempting to make.

First, after Jesus meets the blind man in Bethsaida, he leads him outside the village. Here the reader will recall the inside-outside theme which pervades this Gospel. For Mark, those who are thought to be inside are discovered to be outside, and those who are thought to be outside are discovered to be inside. After the blind man is healed, converted, he is told not to "go into the village" (8:26). Once a person is converted, Mark is saying, he or she cannot go back.

Second, the man comes to see only gradually. Jesus lays his

97

hands on the blind man twice. For Mark, his slow recovery represents the process of conversion for the individual. Belief in Jesus and the acceptance of his way of living and dying and the incorporation of these into a person's lifestyle is a gradual process — not something that takes place overnight.

Also, the blind man is contrasted to the disciples, who are able to see but neither understand nor believe. Mark's portrayal of the disciples is scandalous; they always look foolish; they never seem to understand what Jesus is trying to teach them and they never believe. So, they are contrasted to a blind man, who has never seen Jesus, but who still understands and believes.

The point of the story of the healing of the blind man of Bethsaida, then, is not the healing in and of itself but the gradual conversion process, which must be a part of the life of every person who claims to be a disciple of Jesus.

Meditation: In what ways do you resemble the blind man of Bethsaida? In what ways do you resemble the disciples?

Prayer: God of vision, when your people wandered in the desert, you gave them sight through your servant Moses. When your people strayed from you through sin, you restored them through your prophets. You have given us the vision of your kingdom through Jesus, your Son. Make of us authentic disciples that one day we may see you, Father, Son and Holy Spirit, one God, for ever and ever. Amen.

PIVOT POINT
Mark 8:27-33

Scripture: Jesus turned around and, looking at his disciples, rebuked Peter and said, "Get behind me, Satan. You're not thinking the thoughts of God but as human beings do" (Mark 8:33).

Reflection: The turning point of Mark's Gospel is found in verses 27-33 of chapter eight. In order to understand how these verses are the pivot point, the following observations must be considered.

First, the question and answer session, which introduces this section of the Gospel, is a type of summary of what has gone before. Jesus asks the disciples, "Who do people say that I am ?" (8:27). The question is for the benefit of the reader, who, for the past seven and one-half chapters of the Gospel, has observed Jesus, his disciples, and the crowd interact with each other. Now, an answer must be given to the question.

It is important to note the answers that the disciples relay to Jesus' question, for they are all wrong. While the answers are significant (that is, they are not whimsically chosen by Mark to fill up space on a parchment sheet), they are incorrect.

"John the Baptist" is a good answer. The reader will recall that in the narrative dealing with Herod's fascination with Jesus some people were saying, "John the Baptist has been raised from the dead, and that's why these powers are at work in him" (Jesus)

(6:14). According to Mark, Herod believed that Jesus was John the Baptist come back to life. He said, "It is John whom I beheaded. He has been raised" (6:16). By placing these words on the lips of his Herod, Mark has given the reader a hint of how this Gospel is going to end!

"Elijah" is also a good answer. Again, in the same section mentioned above (6:15), the reader will recall that people thought Jesus to be Elijah, who, it was believed, would return in order to prepare the way for the Messiah. Likewise, the answer, "one of the prophets," echoes the problem of identity as found in the narrative mentioned above (6:15).

Second, once the disciples relay people's answers, which are all wrong, Peter offers the correct reply: "You are the Messiah" (8:29). For the first time in the Gospel, one of the disciples has gotten it right! The reader has to recall that up to this point the demons and everyone else knows who Jesus is except, of course, his disciples.

Third, Mark introduces a new title for Jesus; he refers to him as "Son of Man." This title will be used throughout the second half of the Gospel. It indicates the suffering, rejected, put-to-death, and resurrected Jesus. This is the content of Jesus' teaching in Mark once Peter gets the right answer.

Fourth, the reader suddenly discovers that although Peter has the right answer, he begins to vacilate. This is Mark's way of saying that Peter still has a ways to go. As will be seen throughout the second half of the Gospel, Peter wants a Messiah of power — such as Mark has presented in the first half of his Gospel.

Peter has trouble accepting Jesus' teaching about suffering, rejection, death and resurrection. In fact, he rebukes Jesus for speaking this way. Messiahship, according to Peter — and according to Mark's audience — involved power. Mark is showing that this is a false understanding. Authentic Messiahship, and consequently discipleship, involve powerlessness.

Fifth, Jesus calls Peter "Satan" in the Gospel of Mark. The reader will recall that Jesus has been busy throughout the first half of this Gospel casting out unclean spirits. Now, he identifies another one in his own follower! Peter's confession is declared demonic. He is not thinking as God does — powerlessly — but as human beings do — powerfully.

Not only has Mark suddenly set the stage for the inversion of the whole Gospel, but he has masterfully warned the reader. Mark is cautioning the reader to evaluate his or her answer to the question, "Who is Jesus?" If Jesus' own disciple, Peter, who was known to be the leader of the early Church, could get it all wrong, then what is to keep later followers from arriving at the wrong answer? The stage is now set for Jesus to teach the real meaning of discipleship and the real meaning of conversion to his ways.

Meditation: Who do you say that Jesus is?

Prayer: God of Jesus, in the flesh and blood of the Son of Man you revealed to us the magnitude of your love. Change our hearts to his ways of powerlessness. Strengthen us so that we can follow his way of suffering, rejection, and death, and come to share in his resurrected life. And teach us to think as you do. We ask this through our Lord Jesus Christ, your Son, who lives and reigns with you and the Holy Spirit, one God, for ever and ever. Amen.

POWERLESSNESS

Mark 8:34–9:1

Scripture: "If anyone would be my disciple, he must deny himself, take up his cross and follow me" (Mark 8:34).

Reflection: Jesus' understanding of discipleship in the Gospel of Mark does not consist of power but of powerlessness. Up to Peter's confession about Jesus, Mark has presented a Jesus of power — one who heals the sick, casts out unclean spirits, and works great miracles of feeding thousands of people. This characterization of Jesus is all wrong, Mark states, as he reverses the thrust of the whole first half of the Gospel and begins a new theme of powerlessness.

Authentic discipleship consists of denying self. This is not meant in some masochistic sense, but it does mean that Jesus is the center of a person's life instead of the individual. In the world today, these words fall on deaf ears. Most people today believe that the self comes first and is the center of the universe. Mark teaches that Jesus is the center.

Taking up the cross may not involve carrying a physical piece of wood to the place of execution, as many early Christians did, but it does involve a willingness to stand up to the point of death for what one believes. In the world of today, where many people say what they think another wants to hear in order to get ahead, this teaching is seldom heard.

Following Jesus means being powerless. Authentic power, as Mark understands it and presents it is derived from suffering and death. This is why if a person supposedly saves his or her life, he or she has in fact lost it — for a saved life, one of power, means nothing. But if a person has lost his or her life for the sake of Jesus, this individual has, in fact, saved it and is powerful.

The teaching of Mark's Gospel is difficult for modern people to hear. The usual perception is that God's reality is power, and that the human reality is suffering. Mark reverses these. Throughout the second half of his Gospel, Mark presents the reader with God's reality as being suffering, and the human reality as being power. God, according to Mark, reveals himself in Jesus, who is like us in all things but sin. If we want to know what God is like, Mark is saying, all we have to do is look at Jesus.

Meditation: In what ways do you deny yourself, take up your cross, and follow Jesus?

Prayer: God of Jesus, you have revealed your suffering through the powerlessness of your own Son. He has taught us to deny ourselves, to take up our crosses, and to follow in his steps. Strengthen us in our resolve to be faithful to death so that we might share in the same life of Jesus and the Holy Spirit, who lives and reigns with you, one God, for ever and ever. Amen.

TRANSFIGURATION

Mark 9:2-13

Scripture: He was transformed in front of them, and his clothes became dazzlingly white, so white that no one on earth could bleach them that way (Mark 9:3).

Reflection: Mark's account of the transfiguration of Jesus (borrowed from Mark by both Matthew and Luke) is a masterpiece of writing. It brings together a number of Marcan themes while at the same time setting in motion others, which will be worked out throughout the second half of the Gospel.

First, the narrative functions as a re-commissioning scene. At his baptism by John, Jesus of Nazareth witnesses the opening of the heavens and hears the voice which declares, "You are my beloved Son; in you I am well pleased" (1:11).

The transfiguration account follows Peter's declaration that Jesus is the Messiah, Jesus' rebuke of Peter's attempt to get him to repudiate the cross, his first prediction of the passion, and his teaching concerning authentic discipleship. Jesus is re-commissioned as the "Son of Man," the rejected, suffering, put-to-death, and will-be-raised-to-life Messiah. "This is my beloved Son," the voice from the cloud declares. "Listen to him" (9:7). Hence, Jesus' divinity is re-affirmed, but a new story line is begun for the last half of the Gospel.

Second, this narrative as a whole is a misplaced post-resurrectional account. It contains all the significant details, which the reader should immediately notice.

Mark makes it clear that the transfiguration occurs "after six days." Six is an incomplete number — like the Johannine six stone water jars — which is completed by Jesus. Seven denotes completeness or fullness.

The place for the "event" is a high mountain. Not only did the pagan gods live on mountain tops, but Israel's God seemed to favor certain mountains. It is no accident that two famous "mountain climbers" appear with Jesus. Moses received the law on Mount Sinai, and Elijah heard the tiny, whispering voice there. After the experiences on the mountain, both were sent back down the mountain to God's people to teach them and to lead them. Hence, Mark is stating that Jesus represents both the law and the prophets.

The reader should not miss the three sets of three which appear in the account. Peter, James and John — three persons — accompany Jesus, Moses, and Elijah — three more persons — and Peter wants to make three tents. Three signifies that a theophany is taking place; God is revealing himself.

The post-resurrectional aspect of this account comes through clearly in the detail concerning the dazzlingly white clothes. When the reader gets to the end of the Gospel, he or she discovers that the young man sitting in the tomb is dressed in similar garb. Also, the newly converted and initiated of the early Church wore white. It is through imitating Jesus' example of discipleship that a person shares in new life.

Third, Mark cleverly deals with a concern of his community about the coming of Elijah before the Messiah, a popularly held belief. In Mark, Jesus declares that Elijah has already come in the person of John the Baptizer. By equating Elijah and the Baptizer, the way is now prepared for the Son of Man, who will suffer and be treated with contempt and put to death, just like John the Baptist.

In this section of his Gospel, Mark is asking the reader to

consider a key question, which can be phrased in a number of ways. Is Jesus transfigured because he died on the cross? Will Jesus be raised from the dead because he is transfigured? Does Jesus' power come from his divinity or from his humanity?

By setting up these questions in this section of the Gospel Mark is asking where power, one of his key themes, comes from. We will continue to explore this theme in the days ahead.

Meditation: In what ways have you recently experienced transfiguration?

Prayer: God of conversion, through the suffering, death and resurrection of Jesus you demonstrated your love for all the people of the world. Lead us to your holy mountain. Teach us through your law and your prophets. Enable us to live the baptism which transfigured us into the image of him, who lives and reigns with you and the Holy Spirit, one God, for ever and ever. Amen.

RETALIATION

Matthew 5:38-48

Scripture: "Do not resist the evildoer; on the contrary... Give to those who ask of you... Love your enemies, and pray for those who persecute you so that you may be children of your heavenly Father" (Matthew 5:39, 42, 44-45).

Reflection: The teaching found in the first of five sermons given by Jesus in the Gospel of Matthew continues with selections on retaliation and love of one's enemies. In these sections of the sermon and in sections which precede this one, the law (Torah) is stated and a new interpretation of the law follows.

The unique Matthean arrangement is the author's way of stating that the Torah and the prophets will continue to hold importance for his community. Matthew is not interested in creating a new religion, but he is attempting to show how Jesus continues the original covenant that God initiated with his people. What needs to be completed, in Matthew's understanding, is the "doing" of the commandments.

The challenge facing Matthew's community is that of taking the ancient law and making sense of it in light of this new situation (Jesus as Messiah). The new standard for the "doing" or the keeping of the law is righteousness or authenticity; it consists of behaving in the right way — not for the sake of obedience but for the sake of authenticity, a higher standard.

In the original Israelite culture, the eye-for-an-eye law was considered a moderation in the practice of taking a body for an eye. Righteousness or authenticity, according to Jesus, dictates that not only may one not respond proportionately, but one who wants to fulfill the law, in its spirit as well as its letter, cannot respond at all; he or she cannot resist evil!

Furthermore, righteousness or authenticity demands that a person be like God, who loves everyone — enemies included.

If God, who is perfect, causes rain to fall on the just and the unjust alike, then people are to be like God and love everyone. In other words, God does not judge; God does not separate people into groups of friends and enemies. Therefore, people should not separate people. The separation of one human being from another, according to Matthew's Jesus, is unauthentic behavior.

And behavior is the pivot point for this whole section of the sermon. Matthew is not concerned with dictating specific kinds of conduct; to do this would be to fall back into the trap of the Torah. Matthew is more comfortable giving examples of righteous or authentic behavior, such as offering no resistance to evil, giving away more clothes than what are asked for, walking more miles than requested, loving everyone. Put simply, Matthew's Jesus declares the old law to be too much, but he does not replace or abrogate it with a specific response.

Righteousness dictates that a person may have to go beyond the law, or even break the law, in order to retain his or her righteousness or authenticity. Joseph is held up as this example in the first part of Matthew's Gospel. He breaks the law, takes pregnant Mary as his wife, names the child, and forfeits his state of righteousness — according to the law — in order to do God's will. Sometimes, Matthew is stating, in order to be righteous or authentic, a person must break the law or adhere to a "greater law" — God.

Meditation: In what recent experience did you have to break the law in order to retain your righteousness or your authenticity?

Prayer: God of love, through the ministry of Jesus you have taught your people to do your will. When we are confronted with the evil, help us not to resist. When we are confronted by an enemy, help us to love him or her. Through the working of your Holy Spirit, guide us in your way of righteousness. We ask this through our Lord Jesus Christ, your Son, who lives and reigns with you and the Holy Spirit, one God, for ever and ever. Amen.

INSIDE-OUTSIDE

Mark 2:1-12

SUNDAY
of Week

7

Cycle B

Scripture: So many people gathered around that there was no longer room even in front of the door, and he (Jesus) preached the word to them. Then some people came to him carrying a paralytic, borne by four men. Since they couldn't bring him in because of the crowd, they removed the roof where Jesus was, and after opening it up they lowered the mat on which the paralytic was laid (Mark 2:2-4).

Reflection: In the account of the healing of the paralytic, Mark employs his inside-outside theological image to the fullest. Jesus is "at home"; he is inside. Likewise, there is a large crowd inside with him.

There is one paralytic, however, who is outside. Those who carry him to Jesus want to get him inside. So they remove part of the roof and lower him down into the midst of the crowd. Now, the paralytic is inside. The four men who carried the paralytic look like they are outside but are in fact inside.

The scribes, Mark's adversaries of Jesus, are also inside, but the reader discovers that they are really outside. Their concern is not the healing of the paralytic but the adherence to the law. For Jesus to declare the man's sins forgiven is for Jesus to assume the role of God and thus lay claim to being God. This is blasphemy. This charge will surface later during Jesus' trial before his crucifixion.

It is important for the reader to recall that in the ancient world any kind of disease was attributed to sin, either that of the person himself or herself or his or her parents. The scribes, when confronting Jesus with the charge of blasphemy, provide Jesus with the occasion to challenge this popular notion.

If Jesus cannot forgive the man's sins — as the scribes maintained — then he will simply tell him to pick up his mat and walk. In a touch of Marcan humor, Jesus takes the second route and shows the scribes that the man's paralysis is not due to sin, since no sin is being forgiven. Three interesting points are made by Mark in telling this story.

First, the emphasis is not on the healing of the paralytic, but on the dismantling of the popular notion that illness was caused by sin. Jesus effectively challenges this idea by simply telling the man to pick up his mat and walk.

Second, Mark is placing an emphasis on faith. The faith of the four men, who carry the paralytic and remove the roof and lower him into the house, is spoken of by Jesus. Faith shines outward from within. The faith of others is a powerful force to accomplish good, Mark is saying. Faith motivates people to do good deeds.

Third, healing comes from within. Jesus is within the house. The crowd is within the house. The paralytic is lowered into the house. The scribes look like they are within, but they are really outside. Their concern is not healing. Healing begins within each person and it flows outward — like the healed paralytic who went away in the sight of everyone.

Meditation: In what recent experience have you discovered yourself being healed from within?

Prayer: God of healing, you bring us to birth and care for us throughout the days of our youth. Through the years of adulthood you reveal your healing presence in many and varied ways. Continue to be with us during our life's journey. Forgive the sins we commit, and enable us to glorify you, Father, Son, and Holy Spirit, one God, for ever and ever. Amen

GOLDEN RULE
Luke 6:27-38

Scripture: "As you wish others to do for you, do likewise for them… For with the measure you measure it will be measured out to you in return" (Luke 6:31, 38).

Reflection: As in Matthew's Gospel, in the Gospel according to Luke the section explaining the love of enemies and the exhortation to stop judging others follows the beatitudes. Luke, however, situates the sermon on a plain, while Matthew locates it on a mountain. Luke has four beatitudes with four corresponding woes, while Matthew has nine beatitudes. In Luke, the material following the sermon has been greatly condensed in comparison to the Matthean structure.

Why is there a change in material? The author adjusted the material to fit the needs of his audience. The Gospels are not biographies; they are theological statements, which are addressed to a specific community of people gathered at a particular time in history. Therefore, they reflect only some of the historical situation of Jesus and a lot of the historical situation of the readers.

Matthew addressed a predominantly Jewish-Christian audience. Luke addressed a predominantly Gentile-Christian audience. While locating Jesus' first sermon on a mountain evoked images of Moses and Elijah for Matthew's community, there was no need for Luke to adopt this imagery; a plain was just as good a place as a mountain in order to get similar ideas across.

Likewise, while Matthew could contrast the old law with the new and be understood, Luke's community did not know the old law, so there was no reason for him to refer to it. The teaching of Jesus had to be adjusted to the culture and the mentality of the people who were going to receive it.

Both Matthew and Luke employ the Golden Rule: "Do unto others as you would have them do unto you" (cf. Matthew 7:12; Luke 6:31). This rule is not unique to the Gospels; it is found in both pagan and Jewish sources both before and after the time of the Gospels. But as far as both evangelists are concerned, it serves as a general rule for authentic Christian behavior.

Put simply, authentic Christians, followers of Jesus, when they are ready to act, ask themselves if what they are about to do to others is what they would want to have others do to them. If an honest evaluation is reached, then a person is opened to a wider world of love, lending, mercy, and forgiveness, and a person will more readily respond to the needs of others — even enemies.

Why? Because the Golden Rule is also God's rule. God does to others as he would want them to do to others and, by extension, also to him. "Whatever you do to the least of my brothers, that you do unto me." This can only mean that God behaves toward people as God wants people to behave toward each other and toward him. If a person follows the Golden Rule, he or she acts like God and is a child of the Most High.

This Golden Rule can also be stated in terms of measurement. Just as one measures, so will one be measured. If harsh judgment and lack of forgiveness are used for the measure, then a person will be judged harshly and he or she will not be forgiven. However, if one refuses to judge and is quick to forgive, then he or she will be treated in like manner.

In the ancient world an agreed upon set of measures insured honesty. There was no universally accepted standard of weights and measures as exist today. No one questions the net weight printed on a cereal box or the yard of cloth in a fabric shop. The

Gospel is the standard and Jesus the model upon which we can all agree as Christians. "Judge not lest you be judged." "Forgive and you shall be forgiven." Judgment should not exist among Christians, and lots of forgiveness should always be present.

Meditation: What has been your most recent experience of doing to another as you would have wanted the other to do to you? Or, what has been your most recent experience of receiving in return what you have measured out?

Prayer: God of love, through the teaching of Jesus you instruct us to love our enemies, to do good to those who hate us, to bless those who curse us, and to pray for those who mistreat us. Through the gift of your Holy Spirit, enable us to lend and expect nothing in return, to forgive and to be forgiven, to give and to receive. Through these practices may we receive a good measure, packed together, shaken down, and overflowing and thus come to be like you. We ask this through Christ our Lord. Amen.

TRUST

Mark 9:14-29

Scripture: When Jesus entered the house, his disciples asked him privately, "Why couldn't we drive it out?" And he said to them, "This kind can't be driven out by anything but prayer" (Mark 9:28-29).

Reflection: It's no accident that Mark places the story of the healing of a boy with a "mute spirit" after the segment of the transfiguration and the part about the coming of Elijah and before the second prediction of the passion. The healing of the boy is not the real focus of the story, as Mark narrates it. The major characters in the story are the disciples and the boy's father, and the focus is faith.

The story is not one which illustrates Jesus' power. There is no contest or battle between Jesus and the mute spirit. Jesus simply rebukes the spirit, and it obeys him. The cause for Jesus' action is made clear: the faith of the boy's father.

As Mark portrays the scene, Jesus evokes faith from the boy's father. The man responds with some faith and asks Jesus to supply whatever is missing. Thus, the man is held up to the reader as an example of authentic discipleship.

The boy's father's faith is contrasted to the disciples' lack of faith. Throughout the second half of his Gospel, Mark accents the failure in faith of the disciples. The disciples are unable to drive out the mute spirit because, according to Jesus, they are

117

faith*less*; they do not trust in God. Furthermore, they do not rely on God's power when acting; that is, they do not pray.

In this passage, Mark is questioning the reader about his or her faithfulness and prayer. He is stressing the importance of trust and prayer in the life of a disciple or follower of Jesus. The reader is being asked to identify with either the boy's father or with the disciples.

If the boy's father is chosen, the reader realizes how powerful faith actually is. If the disciples, the usual choice, is made, then the reader discovers the powerlessness of a lack of faith. An interesting thing for the reader to note is how, once Jesus rebukes the mute spirit, the boy is said to look like a corpse, which causes many people to declare, "He is dead!" But Jesus takes him by the hand, raises him up, and gives him back to his father.

Mark is not only giving the reader a clue as to what is going to happen to Jesus, but he is telling the reader of what faith consists — a willingness to die and to be raised to life. Jesus will become like a corpse. The Father will reach out his hand and raise him up. For Mark, faith consists of a willingness to die, to be converted, to get into the tomb, and to trust that the Father will stretch forth his hand and raise one up.

Meditation: Do you identify yourself with the possessed boy's father or with the disciples in this story? Explain.

Prayer: God of faith, throughout history you have invited your people to trust in you. Through your Holy Spirit you give them the right words to call out in prayer to you. Strengthen our trust and fill us with the peace that comes from prayer. Convert us to your ways of life and death. Extend your healing hand and raise us up to share in your life with your Son, our Lord Jesus Christ, who lives and reigns with you and the Holy Spirit, one God, for ever and ever. Amen.

CHILD-LIKE

Mark 9:30-37

Scripture: On the way the disciples had been arguing among themselves about who was the most important... Then he took a child and stood it before them... (Mark 9:34, 36).

Reflection: The second prediction — of Jesus' being "given over into the hands of men," who will "put him to death," and after three days "he will rise" (Mark 9:31) — follows the healing of the boy possessed by a mute spirit and precedes the narrative of the discussion of who is the most important among Jesus' disciples. The placement of these parts of the complete story is no literary accident.

Since Peter's identification of Jesus as the Messiah, the Son of the Living God, and Jesus' rebuke of Peter, the plot of the Gospel takes a turn. Mark has repeatedly told the reader that power does not consist of mighty deeds but of rejection, suffering and death. The disciples, as portrayed by Mark in their discussion of who is the most important, are still interested in their old understanding of power. If they were not, they would not be involved in a discussion about who is the greatest.

In Mark, Jesus explains power as powerlessness in two ways. First, by repeating for the second time his prediction regarding his forthcoming passion and death. Second, by telling the disciples: "If anyone wishes to be first, he must be the last of all and the servant of all" (Mark 9:35).

Following this, a child suddenly appears on the scene. In Jewish culture, there were two groups of people who had no power at all: women and children. So, Jesus chooses a child to represent the most important in the kingdom. This, of course, to the original hearers was a reversal of their cultural values.

By portraying the scene in this way, Mark is declaring that God is like a child — powerless. God is not powerful in the way one usually conceives of power. The reader learns from the child what God is like. Mark is not telling the reader to be childish, but to see in the powerlessness of the child something of a reflection of God's nature.

With this understanding, it is easy to understand why Jesus declares, "Whoever receives one such child in my name, receives me; and whoever receives me, receives not me but the One who sent me" (Mark 9:37). A child is a metaphor for or an image of God. In the kingdom of God, according to Mark, all earthly understandings are reversed.

Meditation: What is your favorite metaphor for or image of God? Does it reflect Mark's understanding in any way?

Prayer: Child-like God, through your own child, Jesus, you have revealed the mystery of your kingdom to all people. When we seek to be first, show us how to be servants of all. When we seek power, show us how to be powerless. Like a trusting child, clear the way so that we may receive Jesus, and in turn receive you, who with Jesus and the Holy Spirit live and reign for ever and ever. Amen.

BELONGING

Mark 9:38-40

Scripture: "Whoever is not against us is for us" (Mark 9:40).

Reflection: In the community for whom this Gospel was written, there was a problem of identity. The problem can be posed as a question: How can a Christian, a follower of Jesus, be recognized? This question can also be phrased slightly differently: What distinguishes a Christian from anyone else?

A short section of Mark's Gospel addresses itself to this question. The section (9:38-41) revolves around the report of an exorcism. The one performing the exorcism was not one of the disciples — meaning that he was not a member of Mark's community. The typical, one might even say the normal, response would be to attempt to stop this person. And indeed Mark's community wanted to do just that.

But Jesus says to them, "Don't stop him. No one who does a mighty work in my name will be able to speak ill of me soon afterwards" (9:39). In other words, a person can be good even though he or she does not belong to the right group. "For whoever is not against us is for us" (9:40).

The reader should recall once again how often Mark makes use of the dichotomy between insiders and outsiders in his Gospel. One of the methods he uses in presenting his characters is to either portray them as inside the right place or outside it. Being inside does not mean that one is a follower of Jesus, and being outside does not mean that one is not a follower of Jesus.

Expanding on this concept we can conclude that there can be good Christians who do not necessarily belong to the right group. They should be allowed to function. In Mark's understanding, there are a variety of ways of following Jesus, and each of these ways is a good way. Whether or not a person belongs to a specific group should not be the criterion for judging his or her authentic discipleship.

Meditation: Name a person you know who is a good Christian but who does not belong to the "right" group. How does this person exercise his or her discipleship?

Prayer: God of all people, you accomplish your will in many and diverse ways through all people. Open our eyes to see the wonders of your love. Open our hearts to the mighty deeds done in your name. Make of us a people who does not exclude others, for in your kingdom there is room for everyone. We ask this through your Son, our Lord Jesus Christ, who lives and reigns with you and the Holy Spirit, one God, for ever and ever. Amen.

GEHENNA

Mark 9:41-50

Scripture: "It is better for you to enter into that life maimed than to go off with two hands into Gehenna, into the un-quenchable fire. It is better for you to enter the kingdom of God with one eye than with two eyes to be thrown into Gehenna, where 'the worm does not die, and the fire is not extinguished'" (Mark 9:43, 47-48).

Reflection: Today, when the word "Gehenna" is heard, it is au-tomatically associated with the word "hell" for most people. However, this is only the last stage in the development of asso-ciations of the word. To better understand Mark's usage of it, the reader must look back through history and understand the de-velopment of the word.

"Gehenna" is a translation of a Hebrew word meaning "Val-ley of Hinnom" or "Valley of the son of Hinnom." It was a valley located southwest of Jerusalem in which there existed an idolatrous cult. One aspect of the ritual of the cult was the sacrifice of chil-dren; children were offered as burning holocausts in the valley.

Once the cult was abolished, some biblical scholars think that Gehenna came to be used as the garbage dump for Jerusa-lem. Such a place would be used not only for garbage but also as the place to leave raw sewage, dead animals, and anything else which might be hauled out of the city. The stench, it is sup-posed, would be far worse than anything emanating from our garbage dumps today.

It is only in New Testament times that Gehenna gets associated with the concept of hell and punishment by fire. This concept itself seems to have come from Jewish apocalyptic literature and was adopted and adapted by Jesus to indicate the fate of those guilty of the most heinous sins and by the early Christians to speculate on what might happen to those who were not faithful.

In employing the image of Gehenna, Mark is following through with his theme of the powerlessness of discipleship imaged in a child. Whoever would lead a child astray — that is, away from faithfulness — would be better off drowned. It is better, according to Mark, to enter the kingdom maimed — powerless — than it is to enter it with all bodily parts — powerful — only to be dumped into Gehenna.

This section of the Gospel is addressed to the disciples, who had been discussing who was the most important among them. The child, an image of powerlessness, is contrasted to the disciples. The child also represents any person who is converted to the Marcan view of discipleship. Furthermore, the child echoes the once-upon-a-time sacrifice of children in Gehenna.

Mark's warning is a stern one: whoever leads a converted disciple astray is not even a good substitute for such a sacrifice. Whoever leads an authentic believer astray is not even good garbage; he or she is not fit for the garbage dump! In other words, such as person cannot get any lower than this.

Therefore, it would be better for one to cut off a hand or foot or to pluck out an eye and take the road of powerlessness in terms of discipleship, than to risk the fires of Gehenna.

Meditation: What are some of your images of discipleship which may conflict with Jesus' image of discipleship?

Prayer: God of the little ones, through Jesus, our teacher and your Son, you have shown us the way to your kingdom. Do not let us wander from your way. Do not let us become insipid. Salt us with the fire of faithfulness of the Holy Spirit, who lives and reigns with you and Jesus, one God, for ever and ever. Amen.

HONOR OR SHAME
Mark 10:1-12

Scripture: Jesus said to them, "Whoever divorces his wife and marries another commits adultery against her; and if she divorces her husband and marries another, she commits adultery" (Mark 10:11-12).

Reflection: The question of divorce was one which fostered a heated debate in Mark's community. It was a question, which, if not answered, had the potential to cause great harm to the community. In the dialogue between Jesus and the Pharisees, who present the question and represent the dictates of the law, the reader witnesses an evolution of the understanding of the permanence of marriage and the equal dignity of man and woman.

The Pharisees are correct insofar as they declare that Moses permitted divorce. A bill of particulars could be drawn up by a married man; if this bill was accepted by the elders, he could divorce his wife.

The reader witnesses the evolution in this thought when Jesus declares, "Moses wrote that commandment for you because of the hardness of your hearts" (10:5). To accuse anyone of "hardness of heart" is to declare that person is totally closed to any further understanding or development.

So we find Jesus here, in Mark's Gospel, declaring that Moses, in permitting divorce, was not reflecting God's will, but was dealing with the "hardness of the people's hearts."

Then he goes on to remind his hearers of the intention of the Creator — in marriage, two become one. Marriage is permanent. That does not mean that in their union the two become one flesh to the point that their individual identities are lost. If anything, in their union they foster the uniqueness of each other and help each other grow as persons.

This understanding of Mark's statement leads directly to the next point in this section of the Gospel. In the culture of the time, a man was the object of honor and a woman, the object of shame. Furthermore, in Judaism only a man, following the law of Moses, could divorce his wife; the wife could not divorce her husband. A woman could divorce her husband only in the Gentile community.

Adultery could be committed only against a man, since another man "used" his property — his wife. Though insulted, the husband, however, could not be shamed, for he was the object of honor. The woman was shamed — and sometimes stoned.

Jesus here reverses all this. He declares that adultery can be committed against the woman, which was impossible in the mentality of the time because the woman had no right to expect her husband's fidelity. And he declares that if the woman divorces her husband and marries another (only in Gentile communities was this possible), she would be committing adultery.

What Jesus has done is to make women objects of honor. He raises women to equal dignity with men. The man and woman in a marriage relationship honor each other. Marriage, according to Jesus, is a relationship of honor. In the kingdom of God, everyone is the object of honor, and no one is the object of shame.

In effect, the question of divorce is not fully resolved here. The discussion moves away from the question of divorce, which is grounded in the context of the Mosaic law, and moves to the equal dignity of man and woman. The question of divorce can be answered only out of this context which, according to Jesus, dates back to "the beginning."

Meditation: In the modern world, who are objects of honor and who are objects of shame? What do you think Jesus would say about this?

Prayer: Honorable God, in the act of creation you formed people in your own image and likeness and bestowed upon them equal human dignity. Through the teaching of Jesus, you have instructed us to honor every person as you do and to shame no one. Help us to recognize inequality and to work toward the elimination of all prejudice. We ask this through our Lord Jesus Christ, your Son, who lives and reigns with you and the Holy Spirit, one God, for ever and ever. Amen.

CHILDREN
Mark 10:13-16

Scripture: People were bringing children to Jesus that he might touch them, but the disciples rebuked them. When Jesus saw this he... said to them, "Whoever does not accept the kingdom of God like a child shall not enter it" (Mark 10:13, 15).

Reflection: Once again, as in chapter nine (vs. 33-36), Mark holds up a child as an image of God and the kingdom. The child, like the woman in the previous account, was powerless and dependent in the culture of Mark's day. There were no child abuse laws or lists of children's rights. The child was property; he or she was owned by his or her father.

Throughout Mark's Gospel, the disciples — all males — are concerned with who is first, the most powerful, the most important in the kingdom, while Jesus is concerned with who is last, least powerful and of no importance in the kingdom. The disciples rebuke those who bring children to Jesus; Jesus, in turn, rebukes the disciples for missing the point; children are examples of what the kingdom of God is like: a community of the powerless.

By portraying Jesus' reaction to children in this way, Mark raises children from a cultural position of shame to one of honor. He takes the powerless and dependent child and holds him or her up as an example of what God is like, of what the kingdom of God is like. Jesus declares that unless a person become as powerless as a child, he or she cannot enter the kingdom of God.

This represents a total reversal of a commonly held presupposition — that the powerful will enter the kingdom. But throughout the second half of his Gospel, Mark has been holding up images of the kingdom which are the exact opposite of what most people think. By doing this, he hopes to jar the reader into conversion.

Meditation: In what ways do you image the kingdom of God? Are your images those of power or powerlessness?

Prayer: God our Father, once you chose a people to be your children. Through Abraham you taught them how to believe. Through Moses you instructed them how to keep the covenant. Through Jesus you have revealed the powerlessness of your kingdom. Help us to accept your kingdom like a child so that we may enter it and share your life with your Son, our Lord Jesus Christ, and your Holy Spirit, who live and reign with you, one God, for ever and ever. Amen.

SEEKING THE KINGDOM

Matthew 6:24-34

Scripture: "First seek the kingdom and the will of God and all those things will be given you besides" (Matthew 6:33).

Reflection: Throughout the first sermon of Jesus (chapters 5-7), Matthew has been dealing with the concept of righteousness. The author has been steering a course between non-abolishment and non-acceptance of the law. This in-between position he calls righteousness.

Matthew's attempt is to steer his audience away from the mere keeping of the law for its own sake while at the same time not abolishing it totally. Therefore, he begins his Gospel with the image of Joseph, a righteous man who retains his righteousness by not following the law and taking Mary as his wife. He does not follow the law precisely in order to do God's will.

In the last section of chapter six of Jesus' first sermon, he speaks of dependence on God. The righteous person, the one who does God's will — no matter what the law dictates — relies on God for food, drink and clothing. This trust in God identifies a person who is righteous, who behaves as God wants, who submits to God's plan of salvation for humankind.

From this perspective, the authentic (just) person realizes that life is more important than food and drink. A lesson of trust can be learned from the birds, who neither sow nor reap, yet they are cared for by God. Therefore, the truly righteous person, who is more important than the birds, trusts God.

Similarly, the wild flowers in the field do not work or spin. Yet, they are clothed in splendor — more than Solomon — by God. The truly righteous person does not worry about clothing because he or she trusts God who holds that people are more important than the wild flowers.

Jesus realizes that all people, no matter whether they are righteous or pagan, need food, drink, and clothing. The difference between the righteous person and the non-righteous individual is this: the righteous person trusts God and seeks the kingdom; he or she does not worry inordinately about food, drink, or clothing. However, the non-righteous or pagan individual is pre-occupied about these things and trusts himself or herself to get them.

Matthew is trying to characterize the attitude of an authentic Christian — great faith in God. This attitude is contrasted to the pagan, who trusts only in himself or herself. Authentic faith is also contrasted to the disciples, who are "of little faith" (6:30). The way of righteousness is a continuous development of a deeper faith in the heavenly Father.

Meditation: In what ways are you dependent on God? In what ways are you dependent on yourself to meet your needs?

Prayer: Heavenly Father, the birds of the sky, who do not sow or reap or gather anything into barns, are fed by you. The wild flowers, who do not work or spin, are clothed in splendor by you. Teach us, who are of little faith, to learn from the birds and the wild flowers how much you care and provide for us. Strengthen our trust in you, and make us righteous so that all things will be given us besides. May we always seek your kingdom, where you live and reign with your Son, our Lord Jesus Christ, and your Holy Spirit, one God, for ever and ever. Amen.

FASTING

Mark 2:18-22

SUNDAY
of Week

8

Cycle B

Scripture: "No one sews a patch of unshrunken cloth onto an old cloak. And no one pours new wine into old wine-skins" (Mark 2:21-22).

Reflection: In Jewish piety, a person fasted in order to demonstrate his or her dependence on God. Fasting was embraced so that one would do without food in order that others could have some food. It was not done for the individual's good but for the sake of others.

The question of fasting is the subject of this section of Mark's Gospel. This sign of Jewish piety was present in the fasting of the disciples of John the Baptist and the disciples of the Pharisees. However, it seems that the disciples of Jesus did not fast. The question that emerges is this: how do the disciples of Jesus demonstrate their dependence on God? This question, of course, is not being asked of the historical disciples but of the members of Mark's community.

In order to dispel the presupposition that fasting demonstrates dependence on God, Jesus employs the metaphor of the wedding feast. During a wedding, the guests do not fast; rather, they engage in eating and drinking. The guests celebrate the marriage with a feast. Once the marriage celebration is concluded, then the practice of fasting can be engaged in again.

This metaphor of bride and bridegroom suggests a new kind of relationship with God. Fasting is not abrogated, but other ways

133

of demonstrating dependence on God are instituted. Borrowed from the prophets' description of the covenant relationship between God and his people, this metaphor on the lips of Jesus speaks of messianic fulfillment, the beginning of something new.

Therefore, to use the old ways of demonstrating dependence on God would be as silly as sewing a new piece of cloth onto an old garment. The strength of the new cloth will pull away from the old and leave a tear which is bigger than before the patch was made. To put this another way, to use the old ways of demonstrating dependence on God would be as silly as pouring new wine into old wineskins. After a few days of fermenting, the gases of the new wine would burst the skins; thus, both wine and skins would be lost.

A new way of demonstrating dependence on God is underway, Mark is saying. New wine must be poured into new wineskins. Jesus represents the fulfillment of the hoped-for Messiah; he, according to Mark, is the bridegroom, and the people are the bride. The wedding feast is in progress in the person of Jesus. Echoes of this theme will be heard later in the two feedings of the multitudes.

Dependence on God is not demonstrated by fasting but by attending the wedding and sharing in the feast. Furthermore, instead of fasting from some food so that others can have some food, at the marriage feast there is plenty of food for everyone. In God's kingdom all people are invited to the eternal marriage feast. The time of preparation is long over; the wedding banquet, which was begun by Jesus, continues.

Meditation: For what reasons do you fast?

Prayer: God of the marriage feast, you began the time of fulfillment in the person of Jesus, the bridegroom of the Church. Guide us in his ways. Do not permit us to patch over the old with the new. Do not permit us to try to store the new in the old. Bring us to a conversion of life that we might share in the eternal wedding banquet with you, Father, Son, and Holy Spirit, one God, for ever and ever. Amen.

TREES AND FRUIT

Luke 6:39-45

Scripture: "A good tree does not bear rotten fruit, nor does a rotten tree bear good fruit. For each tree is known by its own fruit" (Luke 6:43-44).

Reflection: This selection from Luke's Gospel is taken from the sermon of Jesus on the plain. The discussion about trees and their fruit follows the Lucan beatitudes, the woes, teaching about love of enemies, and the teaching about judging others. The context of this particular section of the Gospel is, of course, important.

The sermon is addressed specifically to Jesus' disciples, although a crowd is gathered around. Luke is addressing the leadership of his community through a setting involving disciples. What follows, then, is Luke's characteristics of leadership.

A leader is one with clear vision, according to Luke. He or she cannot be blind. A blind person cannot adequately lead others. Physical blindness, of course, is not the issue. Blindness in the ways of Jesus is the issue. One cannot lead unless one can see the way.

Every leader is trained by Jesus. Therefore, no leader is above Jesus, but, rather, can only teach what he or she has learned.

According to Luke, no leader can judge his followers, since he or she has faults too. To criticize another person for his or her inability to see is to place oneself above the other. Jesus' way is that all people are equal. Leaders are not above their followers.

Every person helps the other to remove whatever it is that blinds him or her. The best way to lead, Luke is saying, is to remember that the follower is like the leader.

The discussion of leadership turns its focus to the relationship between the intention of a person and his or her deeds. A leader is recognized by his or her deeds, much as a tree is recognized by its fruit. If one is able to determine the good tree by its good fruit and the bad tree by its bad fruit, and if one knows what tree to go to pick the fruit for which one is searching, one is also able to point out the best leader. "Each tree is known by its fruit" (6:44). What a leader does is as important as what a leader claims to be.

A good leader reaches into his or her heart where there is a storehouse of goodness, and shares this goodness with those who are led. Similarly, a bad leader reaches into his or her heart, where there is a storehouse of evil, and shares this evil with those who are led. It is "from the abundance of the heart (that) the mouth speaks" (6:45).

In Luke's understanding, leaders in the Church are characterized as people who do not judge their followers, whose vision is that of Jesus, and whose hearts are in harmony with their deeds.

Meditation: What characteristics do you search for in leaders of the Church today?

Prayer: God our leader, through your servants, Moses and Joshua, you led your people to the chosen land. Through your prophets you instructed your people and led them back to you when they had wandered away. Raise up in your Church leaders after your own heart — men and women who possess the vision of Jesus, who lives and reigns with you and the Holy Spirit, one God, for ever and ever. Amen.

RICHES

Mark 10:17-27

Scripture: "Go, sell what you have, and give to the poor and you'll have treasure in heaven; then come, follow me" (Mark 10:21).

Reflection: The story of the rich man, who asks Jesus what he must do to inherit eternal life, echoes the same problems as that of the third type of sown seed in Mark's explanation of the parable of the sower and the seed (4:14-20). The seed sown among thorns "are the ones who hear the word, but worldly cares and the deception of wealth, and desires for all the other things come in and choke the word, and it is unfruitful" (4:18-19). The rich man represents this type of seed.

In the ancient world, being wealthy or rich was considered to be a sign of God's blessing. Any person who was rich was automatically understood to be in high esteem in God's sight, while anyone who was poor was considered to be cursed by God for his or her sin or the sin of his or her parents.

Riches, then, meant power. Those who were rich had the power that the poor could never even think of acquiring. The powerful, rich man in this story leaves saddened. Jesus has told him to reduce his powerful, rich status to that of being poor and powerless. The reader must remember that for Mark power is derived from powerlessness.

No wonder then that the disciples react with amazement

to Jesus' directive to the rich man. Their commonly held and accepted presupposition that wealth indicates a person favored by and secure in God has just been turned upside down.

Why? Riches generate false security. The way to enter the kingdom is not by way of riches or power. The way to enter the kingdom is by way of powerlessness. It is a constant Marcan theme.

Riches comprise a barrier to entrance into the kingdom of God. It is easier to draw a camel through the eye of a needle, as one would thread a needle, than it is for a rich person to get into the kingdom. The rich person relies on his or her riches instead of God.

This representation regarding riches on the part of Jesus is uniquely Marcan. In this passage, you will note, Jesus addresses the disciples as "children" in his response to their amazement. This is no accident. Children, the reader will remember from this and the previous chapter (9-10), represent powerlessness. With the story of the rich man and the address of the disciples as children, Jesus gives the reader a double dose of his understanding of authentic discipleship — being in a shamed (selling all) and powerless (without riches) situation.

Salvation, according to Mark, cannot be earned or bought or manipulated. Neither does salvation consist in the keeping of the commandments, as the rich man has so carefully done from his youth. Salvation is a gift offered by God. So, when the rich man addresses Jesus as "good teacher," Jesus corrects him by saying, "No one is good but God alone" (10:18). God is the source of all goodness. God grants the gift of eternal life.

Meditation: Which of your riches will make it difficult for you to enter the kingdom of God?

Prayer: All good God, all things are possible for you. Instill in us a love for your commandments. Move us to dispossess ourselves of our wealth that we might give all to the poor and have treasure in heaven. We ask this through our Lord Jesus Christ, your Son, who lives and reigns with you and the Holy Spirit, one God, for ever and ever. Amen.

AUTHENTIC
DISCIPLESHIP
Mark 10:28-31

Scripture: "But many who are first will be last, and the last, first" (Mark 10:31).

Reflection: The discussion concerning the difficulty of the rich entering the kingdom of God continues through a statement made by Peter, on behalf of the other disciples, to Jesus: "We have left everything and followed you" (10:28). By portraying Peter in this manner Mark is contrasting discipleship and the rich young man.

However, what the reader suddenly realizes is that the contrast is much like the confrontation between Jesus and Peter on the way to Caesarea Philippi (8:27-33). Peter's statement about having given up everything in order to follow Jesus is another "thinking not as God does but as human beings do" type. Rephrased, Peter is asking, "Are we down far enough yet?"

Jesus' response to Peter demonstrates again of what authentic discipleship consists. It *does* involve giving up house, family, children and land, but for two reasons — for the sake of Jesus and for the sake of the Gospel. Those who have denied themselves these things for these motives are authentic disciples; they have denied themselves for the right reasons.

In Mark's community there were those who were interested in self-denial for the wrong reason — in order to earn their way into the kingdom of God. Discipleship based on this kind of reasoning is not authentic, Mark is saying. Those who look like disciples may not be.

Furthermore, authentic discipleship will be rewarded by God. However, before the reward, the price of discipleship must be paid. Jesus speaks of "persecutions." This is hardly understood as a reward for being faithful to Jesus and the Gospel. Again we see how unlike our way of thinking are the thoughts of God. The way to eternal life — the question with which this section of the Gospel was opened by the rich man — is in God's hands.

Those who in the eyes of the world appear to be first will end up being last. Those who appear to be last will end up being first. In the kingdom of God all is reversed. The authentic disciple recognizes this, Mark is saying, and, instead of being concerned about a reward, focuses on being faithful to Jesus and the Gospel.

Meditation: Are you a disciple of Jesus in order to receive a reward, or are you a disciple of Jesus for his sake and that of the Gospel? Explain.

Prayer: God of the kingdom, you take the first and make them last, and you take the last and make them first. Instill in us the spirit of authentic discipleship through the working of your Holy Spirit. Keep us faithful to Jesus and to the Gospel. Enable us to believe that with you the impossible is always possible. We ask this through Christ our Lord. Amen.

SHARING THE CUP
Mark 10:32-45

Scripture: "Whoever would be great among you must be your servant; and whoever would be first among you must be the slave of all. For even the Son of Man came, not to be served but to serve, and to give his life as a ransom for many" (Mark 10:43-45).

Reflection: Jesus' third prediction of his passion in the Gospel of Mark and the dialogue between Jesus, James and John follow the discussion of the difficulty of the rich to enter the kingdom of God and Peter's misunderstanding concerning a reward for having given up everything to follow Jesus. In this section of the Gospel, Mark reaches a climax in his theme that power for God is powerlessness.

The third prediction of the passion focuses on Jesus' imminent entrance into Jerusalem. There, the Son of Man, Mark's designation for powerlessness, will be handed over "to the chief priests and the scribes. They'll condemn him to death and hand him over to the Gentiles who'll mock him and spit on him and scourge him and kill him; but after three days he will rise" (10:33-34). Not only does Mark re-emphasize the powerlessness of Jesus here, but he also summarizes the concluding chapters of his Gospel. Using this literary device (foretelling), he tries to keep the reader interested until the end of the story.

From the very beginning of the Gospel, Mark has portrayed

the disciples as being somewhat dense. And from the time of Peter's rebuke at Caesarea Philippi they have only grown in their misunderstanding of what Jesus has been trying to teach them. That misunderstanding reaches a climax when James and John ask for positions at the right and the left of Jesus, when he comes into his glory. They are asking for positions of power.

Jesus has just finished speaking about powerlessness, but they still do not get it — they are still interested in power.

It is a message addressed in a special way to the people of Mark's time, his audience. Mark's readers were attempting to turn discipleship into positions of power. In the way he wrote his Gospel, Mark shows that he wants his community to realize that following Jesus — discipleship — is the exact opposite of what they think it is.

This discussion of power is similar to the discussion of who is the most important (9:33-36), which began this section of the Gospel. Instead of a child being brought in as a sign of powerlessness, Mark introduces the Old Testament metaphor of "drinking of the cup." To drink of the cup is to accept one's destiny as assigned by God. In Jesus' case, this means suffering, death and resurrection.

The disciples can participate in this through baptism. The baptism spoken of here by Jesus is not the baptism he received at the hands of John in the Jordan River. This baptism will take place through Jesus' crucifixion and death. If his disciples want to share in Jesus' glory, like James and John, they must first of all share in his death and resurrection.

This was done in the early Church, and continues to be practiced today, through the celebration of the Eucharist. The Eucharist is the celebration of the death of Jesus. Followers of Jesus drink from the cup, and thus participate in his death; they are baptized with the baptism as he was.

If this participation in the suffering and death of Jesus is understood, then the question of authority is mute.

Jesus points out in the Gospel of Mark that the Gentiles have a hierarchical system of governing consisting of the rulers and those who are ruled. It cannot be that way among the followers of Jesus. Whoever is greatest among them must be a servant of the rest; whoever is first must be a slave. Why? Because the Son of Man made himself both servant and slave. His followers, if they are to be authentic, must imitate his life and drink from his cup.

For Mark, the understanding of authentic discipleship is complete. Power, authority, and honor have been discussed and contrasted. Those who follow the Son of Man suffer, welcome children, uphold the dignity of women, and practice poverty. Those who follow the way of the world seek power, honor, comfort and riches. Mark's readers (disciples) are encouraged to follow the Son of Man.

Meditation: Are you a disciple of the world or of the Son of Man? Explain.

Prayer: God of servants, through the Gospel you teach us a way of powerlessness in the handing over, condemning, mocking, spitting upon, scourging, and death of your Son, Jesus. Baptize us into your way. Share with us the cup of Jesus. Form us into servants and slaves that one day we may share in your greatness in the kingdom where you live and reign as Father, Son, and Holy Spirit, one God, for ever and ever. Amen.

SON OF DAVID

Mark 10:46-52

Scripture: "Jesus, son of David, have mercy on me. Master, I want to see" (Mark 10:47-51).

Reflection: The narrative of the healing of the blind Bartimaeus functions both as a commentary on the preceding section of Mark's Gospel (8:22-10:45), which began with the healing of the blind man of Bethsaida, and as an introduction to the account of Jesus' entry into Jerusalem. In other words, the healing of Bartimaeus is like a hinge for this part of the Gospel.

Bartimaeus in this passage is being contrasted to the disciples. He is physically blind but he sees; they are blind in terms of understanding what Jesus has been teaching them about the powerlessness of authentic discipleship, but they do not see. Bartimaeus believes; his faith saves him. The disciples do not believe; they have not yet professed belief in Jesus' way.

Furthermore, Bartimaeus follows Jesus. He professes faith and follows him on the way. The disciples, as Mark will portray them later, abandon Jesus all together. Bartimaeus responds to Jesus' call with discipleship; the disciples do not.

This story, then, functions as a warning to those who claim to be authentic disciples of Jesus. Mark is questioning faith and discipleship. He is asking his readers to look into themselves and to determine if they are really "inside" or if they only look like they are "inside." The reader must recall that throughout the

145

Gospel Mark has demonstrated that those who look like they are "inside" may, in fact, be on the "outside," and those on the "outside" may really be "inside."

Also, a new title is given to Jesus in this section: Son of David! This title will be echoed in the next section of the Gospel as Jesus makes his entry into Jerusalem. The crowd that accompanies him call out, "Blessed is the coming kingdom of our Father David!" (11:10). The entry into Jerusalem begins the story of the last seven days of Jesus' life in Mark's Gospel.

The entry into Jerusalem (11:1-10), which is omitted from the semi-continuous weekday cycle, begins the saving act of Jesus. Mark echoes this in the last line of the story concerning the ambition of James and John: "The Son of Man came, not to be served, but to serve, and to give his life as a ransom for many" (10:45). It is also echoed in the healing of Bartimaeus account, when Jesus declares, "Your faith has saved you" (10:52).

For Mark, Jesus is the ransom, the pledge set to buy back slaves. Jesus will redeem all slaves. Jesus will save the powerless, those who are held in bondage. Mark's Gospel turns its focus in this direction for the next six chapters.

Meditation: In what ways have you responded to Jesus' call to discipleship?

Prayer: God of light, Jesus, the Son of David, opened the eyes of the blind in order that all men and women might see you and believe. When we are blinded by worldly concerns, open our eyes to the wonders of your grace. When we fail to answer your call, guide us to your side. When we falter in the ways of discipleship, strengthen us through the working of your Holy Spirit, who lives and reigns with you and our Lord Jesus Christ, one God, for ever and ever. Amen.

FIG TREE
Mark 11:11-26

Scripture: Jesus was hungry. And seeing from a distance a fig tree which had leaves on it, he went over to see if he could find anything to eat, but when he came up to it he found it had nothing but leaves, because it wasn't the season for figs. And in response he said to it, "May no one eat fruit from you ever again!" (Mark 11:12-14)

Reflection: The entry into Jerusalem has been accomplished. The Son of David has been greeted with "Hosanna in the highest!" (11:10). During the first day of his last seven days, Jesus enters the Temple area, but, "since it was by now the evening hour, he went out to Bethany with the Twelve" (11:11).

For Mark this is an allegorical statement. He is declaring that the time of the Temple is over. Jesus is the Son of David, who has entered a dying Jerusalem. Here we find some of Mark's irony at its best. It is re-emphasized in the narrative of the next day's events, especially the story about the cursing of the fig tree.

Like the fig tree, which has nothing but leaves, that is, is barren, so is the official Temple worship in Mark's understanding. It is not possible to reform it, as it is not the proper time or season. Therefore, the Temple will be destroyed.

So, Jesus enters and begins its dismantling by driving out those selling and buying there, by overturning the tables of the money changers and the seats of those who were selling doves.

By the time that Mark wrote this Gospel, the Temple had already been destroyed by the Romans in 70 A.D. Mark is attempting to explain why he thinks the Temple was destroyed: it no longer served its purpose as a place where God was to be worshiped. It was barren of true worshipers.

The authentic follower of Jesus is able to produce fruit out of season, according to Mark. One who follows Jesus is not like the fig tree, which only produces fruit at a certain time of the year. Jesus expects fruit when he demands it. Jesus expects conversion.

Like the Temple, which is cleansed or exorcised by Jesus, so the individual Christian must be cleansed, converted. "My house shall be called a house of prayer for all the nations," Jesus quotes the prophets. The last time prayer was mentioned in Mark's Gospel was in the incident where the disciples were unable to cast out an unclean spirit. Jesus declared that it could be done only with prayer.

Prayer replaces the Temple. All nations, which means the Gentiles, can be converted. Prayer, for Mark, becomes the new Temple. Whatever is asked for in prayer, if the petitioner believes, will be received. One can approach God directly in prayer; the day of the Temple is gone.

The Son of David has entered Jerusalem and, on the first of the last seven days of his life, declared the Temple null and void. On the second of these last days, he exorcised the Temple and declared that the authentic Christian (represented by the fig tree) has no need of a Temple for worship. A Christian should be bearing fruit whenever it is needed.

The encounter of the withered and cursed fig tree opens the scene on the third day. Jesus declares that the necessity of worship in the Temple no longer exists; now, each person can deal directly with God through prayer.

Meditation: In what ways does your personal prayer characterize your relationship with God?

Prayer: God of the covenant, you established the house of your servant, David, in Jerusalem, and you promised that an heir would rule upon his throne. In the fullness of time you kept your promise by sending Jesus, your Son, who established a new and lasting covenant through his own blood. Make us true and authentic followers of him, that we might be fruitful in season and out of season. We ask you to hear us through the same Christ our Lord. Amen.

AUTHORITY
Mark 11:27-33

Scripture: As Jesus was walking about in the Temple area, the chief priests, the scribes, and the elders came up to him and said, "By what authority do you do these things? Who gave you the authority to do them?" (Mark 11:27-28).

Reflection: Following the episode of the withered tree and Jesus' exhortation concerning prayer, Jesus and the disciples return to Jerusalem and the Temple for the next scene during the third of the last seven days recounted in Mark's Gospel. The topic of this first encounter in the Temple is authority. The first half of the section is composed of a riddle; the second half consists of the parable of the tenants.

The question of Jesus' authority echoes the first part of Mark's Gospel, wherein those in authority (Pharisees) constantly question Jesus' behavior of eating with sinners and tax collectors, not fasting, picking heads of grain on the Sabbath, curing on the Sabbath, etc. In all of these incidents the reader discovers that Jesus has no authority in the Jewish understanding of the term; that is, Jesus has not been trained by another recognized rabbi or teacher. This question was most likely one with which the early Church struggled in its quest for its own identity and legitimacy.

Remembering one of Mark's major themes — no sign can be given for faith — the reader immediately notices that the chief priests, the scribes, and the elders ask Jesus for a sign of his authority. The request for a sign is countered by a riddle: "John's baptism, was it from heaven or was it of human origin?" (11:30). The riddle reflects Mark's community's efforts to deal with the authority question for itself.

If the reader, like the questioners, answers that John's baptism was of heavenly origin, then he or she is faced with the fact that he or she did not believe in John. In other words, if John had authority, then why not believe in him?

If, on the other hand, the reader, like the questioners, answers that John's baptism was of human origin, then those who thought that John was a prophet would rise up against those who do not believe. In other words, if John had no authority, how does the reader explain the great numbers of people who went to him for baptism?

The riddle is left unsolved. Jesus needs no sign of authority to do the things he does. According to Mark, the person who looks for a sign in order to profess faith looks for the wrong thing. There can be no sign, as far as Mark is concerned. "No sign will be given to this generation" (8:12). A person either believes or he or she does not.

With this said, the tables will be turned on the questioners. In the parable of the tenants, Jesus will question their authority and show them that it is illegitimate.

Meditation: What or who comprises all the various authorities in your life? Make a list.

Prayer: God of authority, from the moment of your silent conception in the womb of the Blessed Virgin Mary to the day of your ignominious death on the cross, you constantly care for your people. Through the gift of your Holy Spirit, guide our daily deeds. May we do only that which pleases you and gives you glory through our Lord Jesus Christ, who lives and reigns with you and the Holy Spirit, one God, for ever and ever. Amen.

HEARING AND ACTING

Scripture: "Everyone who hears these words of mine and acts on them is like a wise man who built his house on rock… Everyone who hears these words of mine but does not act on them is like a foolish man who built his house on sand" (Matthew 7:24, 26).

Reflection: The comparison of those who listen to the words of Jesus and act on them to the man who built his house on rock and the comparison of those who listen to the words of Jesus but do not act on them to the man who built his house on sand concludes the first sermon in Matthew's Gospel.

First, the narrative is addressed to the reader, who has been listening to (reading) the words of Jesus for the last three chapters. The reader has a choice: he or she can act on these words or not act on them. The person who chooses to act on or practice the words which have been heard is the shrewd or wise one, who is secure and steady as a rock. The person who chooses not to act on or practice the words, which have been heard, is the fool, the one who cannot figure out what to do, who shifts like sand.

It is important to note that both types of people have heard the words of Jesus. The decision they must make is whether or not to act on these words. According to Matthew, it is up to the wise or shrewd person to figure out what to do, how to practice the words of Jesus.

Second, Matthew is not only summarizing the whole first sermon of Jesus, but he is addressing those who are already in the fold of early Christianity, those who already believe. The question he is trying to answer is this: What does one do with what one has heard? In other words, how does one put into practice the words of Jesus?

Throughout this first sermon, Jesus has given a new interpretation of the Torah. The author believes that the words of Jesus form a true interpretation of the old law. Followers of Jesus must respond to this new interpretation and do something with it; that is, followers of Jesus must build the edifice of their lives on the rock of Jesus' teaching. To do so indicates that one has heard and that one is acting on what has been heard.

Third, then when the rains of doubt come, when the floods of persecution appear, when the winds of anger blow and buffet one's house, it will not collapse; it is set solidly on rock. If however, the house is built on sand, when doubts, persecution, and anger arise, it will collapse and be ruined. For Matthew, the house is each person.

Fourth, throughout this first sermon of Jesus, Matthew has reinterpreted the Torah for his community. However, he has never specified of what the best action consists. He cannot do this. If he did, he would be establishing a new law, which he does not want to do. This is what everyone hears, but only the shrewd, those who are able to determine what correct behavior is, what the will of God is, build their houses on rock.

Meditation: In what ways is your house built on rock? In what ways is your house built on sand?

Prayer: God our rock, once you chose a people and, through your servant David, built a house for them. From this house was born Jesus, your eternal word. May we always listen to his words and, through practice of them, build our house on doing your will. We ask this through our Lord Jesus Christ, who lives and reigns with you and the Holy Spirit, one God, for ever and ever. Amen.

SABBATH

Mark 2:23-3:6

Scripture: "The Sabbath was made for man, not man for the Sabbath" (Mark 2:27).

Reflection: The discussion concerning the observance of the Sabbath between Jesus and the Pharisees is composed of two stories — the disciples picking grain and the healing of a man with a withered hand.

The Pharisaic tradition viewed the Sabbath as a day framed in rules to be strictly observed. Through careful observance of the law, a person demonstrated his or her adherence to the ways of God. Therefore, everything — including how far one could walk and what one could do — was regulated.

Within this type of Sabbath observance, it was easy to forget the true intent of the origin of the Sabbath. It was not instituted as a day set aside for legal observance in honor of God; it was begun as a day of rest for the people of Israel. During a time of leisure, the people were to remember and celebrate all that God had done for them.

Jesus reminds the reader of this fact in the Gospel of Mark: people were not made for the Sabbath, the Sabbath was made for them. The rules governing the Sabbath can be broken in cases of necessity. When people are hungry, they need to gather food. When David, the greatest of Israel's kings, and his men were hungry, they ate of the forbidden bread of the Temple. Human need overrode the Sabbath; an exception was made for human beings.

Likewise, a person who needs to be healed cannot wait until the Sabbath is over. "Is it lawful to do good on the Sabbath or to do evil, to save life or to destroy it?" Jesus asks (3:4). The answer is obvious: one does good and one saves life because both of these are more important than the Sabbath.

The question of the Sabbath is placed into a wider context by Mark. The reader is challenged to evaluate the intent of the Sabbath regulation. In this passage, Jesus places people and their needs — the original intent of the Sabbath — before the rules governing the Sabbath's observance. Furthermore, he claims authority to do this by declaring, "The Son of Man is Lord even of the Sabbath" (2:29).

This conflict between Jesus and the Pharisees will reappear in the Gospel in chapters eleven and twelve. After entering Jerusalem, he engages in a series of debates with the Pharisees and the Herodians. When Mark states, "The Pharisees left and at once began to plot with the Herodians to do away with Jesus" (3:6), he is preparing the reader for the final conflict, which will bring Jesus to death.

Through these series of conflict stories, which reflect a similar pattern — statement of fact, question of protest, reply by Jesus — Mark not only illustrates the problems which were facing his own community, but he also teaches his reader the meaning of converting to Jesus' ways.

Meditation: In which ways do you observe the Sabbath (Sunday) by putting people first and by observance of the law?

Prayer: God of the Sabbath, you gave your people a day of rest from labor that they might remember and celebrate your mighty deeds. Guide us in upholding the dignity of all people. Never let us forget the salvation that you have accomplished for us in Jesus Christ, your Son and Lord of the Sabbath, who lives and reigns with you and the Holy Spirit, one God, for ever and ever. Amen.

GENTILE MISSION
Luke 7:1-10

SUNDAY
of Week

9

Cycle C

Scripture: "I tell you, not even in Israel have I found such faith" (Luke 7:9).

Reflection: The account of the healing of the centurion's slave in Luke functions as a preparation for the conversion of Cornelius, a Roman centurion, in Luke's second volume, the Acts of the Apostles. Therefore, the emphasis of the story is placed on the positive qualities of the Gentiles. Luke is attempting to justify the mission to the Gentiles.

By the time of Luke's Gospel (80-90 A.D.), the early Church had moved into the Gentile world. Gentiles were converted and large communities of Gentile-Christians began to spring up around the Mediterranean Sea. Luke, as well as the other Gospel writers, had to deal with the fact that Jesus probably did not minister to the Gentiles. Therefore, in an attempt to demonstrate the growing belief that Jesus had to come to save all people, the writers of the Gospels were inspired to portray Jesus with a positive attitude toward the Gentiles.

Luke's version of the healing of the centurion's slave reflects this positive thrust toward Gentiles, especially when the reader remembers that the centurion represents the Roman occupation forces of the Jewish homeland. To portray anything positive about the Roman occupation forces is to risk losing a Jewish audience. Since Luke's audience is probably primarily Gentiles, he has little to lose.

Jews approach Jesus and deliver the message of the illness of the centurion's slave. It seems that Luke has forgotten the old hostility between a conquered people and the conquerors. Furthermore, the centurion loves the Jewish nation and has helped build their synagogue. The centurion could hardly be presented in a more positive light.

The centurion knows the Jewish law concerning the resulting uncleanness upon entering the house of a Gentile, so he sends friends to tell Jesus that he is unworthy to have Jesus enter his house. Typical of Luke, the centurion's friends relay the message, "Just say the word and my servant will be healed" (7:7). The "word" — in the form of preaching and teaching — is the foundation of Luke's Gospel.

The Roman centurion (a commander of a hundred men), who represents the occupation forces and who thus has authority over others, submits himself to Jesus' authority. He knows how to use authority, but he chooses to submit himself to the authority of Jesus. In this way, Luke masterfully demonstrates the submission and conversion of the Gentiles. This Roman centurion becomes a model for other Gentiles.

The point of the story, as far as Luke is concerned, is not the healing of an ill slave. The focus is on the evangelization of the Gentiles as contrasted to the lack of belief on the part of the Jews. Luke is not castigating the Jews, but he does know that Jesus was not accepted by his own people. Luke is attempting to uphold the legitimacy of the mission to the Gentiles and its positive results.

"God doesn't play favorites," Peter states in the Acts of the Apostles before he baptizes Cornelius. "Instead, those of every nation who fear him and do what is right are acceptable to him" (Acts 10:34-35).

Meditation: Which people (who may be considered to be the enemy or oppressors — personally or nationally) are waiting to hear the good news preached to them?

Prayer: God of every nation, you show no partiality, but you invite all people to fear you and to do what is right before you. Through Jesus, who became like a slave for us, you brought all people together as one. Fill us with your Holy Spirit, that we might never fail in sharing this good news with all we meet. Make us messengers of your word that we might proclaim peace through Jesus Christ, your Son, who is Lord of all, for ever and ever. Amen.

HISTORY OF SALVATION
Mark 12:1-12

Scripture: "What, then, will the lord of the vineyard do? He'll come and do away with the farmers and give the vineyard to others" (Mark 12:9).

Reflection: The third of the last seven days of Jesus' life in Mark's Gospel continues with the parable of the tenants. The Gospel writer is, obviously, the author of the parable, since it functions as a summary of salvation from the choice of Israel to the ingathering of the Gentiles. In the Marcan context, the parable functions as a riddle; however, it does not confuse anyone.

The setting is a vineyard, which is protected by a hedge and a tower and is fully equipped with a wine press. The vineyard metaphor, borrowed from the Old Testament, represents Israel, God's chosen people. The man who plants the vineyard is, of course, God himself. The tenant farmers are the religious leaders of Israel.

For Mark, these leaders are represented under the collective name of "Pharisees." The vineyard owner's servants are the prophets, who have been sent throughout time and always met with death. Their message — reform — was seldom heeded.

The son of the vineyard owner is Jesus. He is the heir of the vineyard (the kingdom). He will be killed (in the context of the plot of Mark's Gospel) and the vineyard will be given to others. These others are the Gentiles.

The reader knows the meaning of the parable: God's covenant has been transferred from the Israelites to all people of faith. Because of Jesus, everyone is a part of the vineyard.

Furthermore, the religious leaders (Pharisees, for Mark) are punished. The tenants are put to death. Their authority is shown to be illegitimate. Legitimate authority resides in Jesus, the one who will suffer, die, and rise. His authority is unchallenged.

Meditation: Today, what appropriate metaphors can be used to summarize the history of salvation?

Prayer: God of the vineyard, once you drove away nations and transplanted a vine from Egypt. You cleared the ground for it; it took root and filled the land. Those to whom you leased it have broken down its walls and laid it waste. Look down from your heaven and see us: take care of your vine and protect what your right hand has planted. May all people come to realize the new life that you give through your Son, our Lord Jesus Christ, who lives and reigns with you and the Holy Spirit, one God for ever and ever. Amen.

TAXES

Mark 12:13-17

Scripture: "Render to Caesar the things that are Caesar's and to God the things that are God's" (Mark 12:17).

Reflection: The third of Jesus' last seven days in the Gospel of Mark continues with the question about paying taxes to the emperor.

The question is an explosive one, when the reader considers that the Pharisees, who did not favor the tax, and the Herodians, who did favor payment of the tax, both present themselves to Jesus. No matter what answer Jesus gives, he is trapped. Jesus will either end up taking a position contrary to that held by most of the Jews (it is unlawful to pay the tax) or one which will bring him in conflict with the Roman authorities (it is lawful to pay the tax).

However, the theological question, with which Mark is attempting to deal, has nothing to do with taxes. The underlying theological debate has to do with the presupposition of the existence of two kingdoms — that of God and that of the emperor. If the questioner posits the existence of two kingdoms, which one has legitimate authority, and which one has power?

Those who ask this legal question produce the Roman coin when Jesus asks for it. Since the questioners possess and use the coin themselves, it is obvious that they see some benefit in it. In effect, they have accepted the financial advantages of the Roman administration of the land. By the fact that they possess the coin, the questioners have answered their own question. It is not a matter of two kingdoms. Those who use Caesar's money should pay his taxes.

Those who share in the fruits of the vineyard (cf. the parable of the tenants — Mark 12:1-12) should give to God what belongs to him. Caesar's coin is temporary; all else is eternal and belongs to God. God's image and inscription are not found on coins but on all of creation.

By answering in this way, Jesus avoids taking sides and exposes the hypocrisy of those who ask the question. It is not a question of paying or not paying the tax; it is a question of where one's loyalties lie in actual fact.

Meditation: In what ways do you give to the government what belongs to the government and to God what belongs to God?

Prayer: God of truth, you alone possess sole authority over heaven and earth. Bless those who have been entrusted with the leadership of nations. Guide them in pursuit of the common good. Never let us forget that all human governments are subject to the laws of your kingdom, where you live with our Lord Jesus Christ and the Holy Spirit, one God, for ever and ever. Amen.

RESURRECTION

Mark 12:18-27

Scripture: "Haven't you read in the scroll of Moses, in the passage about the thorn bush, how God spoke to him, and said, 'I am the God of Abraham and the God of Isaac and the God of Jacob'? He's not God of the dead but of the living" (Mark 12:26-27).

Reflection: Into the middle of the debates between Jesus and those in authority (usually represented by the Pharisees) Mark inserts two points of agreement between Judaism and nascent Christianity. The first area of agreement concerns the resurrection; the second has to do with which commandment is the greatest, a matter which is treated in tomorrow's selection.

While the Sadducees do not believe in resurrection, the Pharisees do. The question posed by the Sadducees is one which was often debated. Moses had ordered that if a man died and left no heir, his brother should marry his widow and his brother's child would be considered the dead man's descendant. This practice insured family continuity. If seven brothers married the same woman, whose wife will the woman be on the day of resurrection?

Jesus does not fall into the trap. The question makes the issue of resurrection rather ridiculous. The Sadducees, who do not believe in resurrection, know this. What Jesus does, however, is to raise the question to a different level. The point, according to him, is not to whom will the woman be married ("when you rise from the dead, you neither marry nor are given in marriage" — 12:25), but that God is the God of the living.

The Sadducees, who have quoted the Old Testament, are accused of not knowing either the Scriptures or the power of God. The commonly held notion was that those raised from the dead would continue a life much like the one they had before death. Jesus declares that no one knows what the resurrection of the dead is like. However, any sexual relationships of this world will be transcended. Those who rise will be the creative work of the power of God.

God is the God of the patriarchs, who died centuries ago. Since God identifies himself in relationship to them, and because of their relationship to him, they are alive. God is the God of the living. He has the power to give life to all. He is not limited through marriage in sharing life, as are people. God transcends human ways of giving life.

Thus, on this third of the last seven days of Jesus' life in Mark's Gospel, Mark makes it clear that both Pharisees and Christians basically agreed on this most critical issue — resurrection. It will be necessary for Mark (and especially Matthew and Luke) to distinguish the differences; this will be done through a series of stories about the empty tomb (Mark, Matthew, and Luke) and resurrection appearances of Jesus after he rose from the dead (Luke).

Meditation: What beliefs do both Jews and Christians share today?

Prayer: God of Abraham, Isaac, and Jacob, you have always called people to share in your life. You, the God of the living, promise to raise up to new life those who follow your ways. Be with us throughout life's journey. Guide us with your Holy Spirit. Bring us at last to the fullness of life, which you share with your Son, our Lord Jesus Christ, one God for ever and ever. Amen.

LOVE

Mark 12:28-34

Scripture: "You are not far from the kingdom of God" (Mark 12:34).

Reflection: The question of the greatest or the first of all of the commandments of the law was a regularly disputed question in Judaism, especially in the Talmud, the commentary on the law. Therefore, while it is a legitimate question, it is also one that can cause problems.

The Marcan Jesus answers the questioning scribe by reciting the Shema, a Jewish prayer said three times every day: "Hear, O Israel! The Lord your God is Lord alone! You shall love the Lord your God with all your heart, with all your soul, with all your mind, and with all your strength" (12:29-30). In other words, the love of God must be the object of the total person — heart, soul, mind, strength. At this point in the narrative, it is obvious that Jesus and Judaism are in agreement.

However, Jesus does not give a single answer to the question about the greatest or first of the commandments. Quoting the book of Leviticus, Jesus declares, "You shall love your neighbor as yourself" (12:31). Then, "There is no other commandment greater than these" (12:31).

Jesus has gone beyond the range of the original question. To the greatest or first commandment is added a second — the love of neighbor. These are not two commandments but one. The

Marcan Jesus identifies the love of God with the love of neighbor. A person loves God to the extent that he or she loves others. A person loves others to the extent that he or she loves God. The two cannot be divorced.

This union of these two commandments is something new. Generally, it was understood in Judaism that one could love God without any overt concern for others and self. Likewise, one could love others and self without any great love of God.

The division was much like that which exists today for those who practice religion for one hour a week and claim "faith" while participating in gossip, illegal deals, and never reaching out to help others.

By going beyond the extent of the original question, Jesus has declared the question itself invalid. There is no greater commandment than the one to love, for it summarizes all of the commandments.

The scribe, who is declared to be "not far from the kingdom of God" (12:34), represents Mark's theological position. Mark wants to preserve a link between Judaism and Christianity; he does not want to begin a new religion. The best way to accomplish this is to portray Jesus as merging two Jewish texts, which results in a new understanding: the love of God, neighbor, and self are intertwined. The person who hears, understands, and practices this is "not far from the kingdom of God."

Meditation: How far are you from the kingdom of God?

Prayer: God of love, you guide all of creation with your commandment of love. Help us to love you with all our heart, our soul, our mind, and our strength. Help us to love our neighbor as we love ourselves. By doing so, may we come to share in the kingdom, where you live and reign with your Son, our Lord Jesus Christ, and your Holy Spirit, one God, for ever and ever. Amen.

SERVANTS

Mark 12:35-37

Scripture: "How can the scribes say that the Messiah is the son of David?" (Mark 12:35)

Reflection: The teaching in the Temple continues on the third of the last seven days of Jesus' life in the Gospel according to Mark with the presentation of a problem that confounded Mark's community. The problem is this: How can the Messiah be a descendant (son) of David, if David himself calls him Lord (Master) in Psalm 110:1? We heard Jesus being called the son of David by blind Bartimaeus (10:47) and by the crowd as he entered Jerusalem (11:10). As can be seen, the Davidic (and even the divine) origin of the Messiah is the question.

The Messianic expectation revolved around a descendant (son) of David. The Messiah was expected to be a warrior-king like David, the prototype of the savior. David, the reader must remember, had extended the borders of Israel as far as they had ever been pushed back, and he gave the people a period of unity and peace.

So, if David calls his son "Lord" (Master), can the Messiah be a son of David who, in referring to the Messiah as Master, is implying that he is a slave? A slave (David) cannot be greater than his Master (the Messiah), yet the Master (the Messiah) is a descendant (son) of David.

Mark resolves this problem for his community by reducing everyone to the status of a slave. According to Mark, everyone is powerless; every person is dependent upon every other individual. "If anyone wishes to be first, he must be the last of all and the servant of all" (9:35), Jesus tells the Twelve after they argue about who is the most important.

James and John want the first places on the right and the left sides of Jesus, when he enters into his glory. Jesus tells them, "Whoever would be first among you must be the slave of all" (10:43-44). Then, the answer to the question, which has been dealt with in this section of the Gospel, is given before the question is asked: "For even the Son of Man came, not to be served, but to serve, and to give his life as a ransom for many" (10:45).

David is correct in calling the Messiah his Master, for David was a slave of God (the Messiah). It is also correct to refer to Jesus as the son of David, for he, too, was a slave, a servant of those he came to save. In effect, there are no Masters — only slaves — as far as Mark is concerned.

This answer to this question, which is predicated of the scribes, indicates that in the early Church, both Judaism and Christianity accepted the presupposition that the Messiah (Christ) was a descendant (son) of David.

Meditation: In what ways are you a slave? In what ways are you a master?

Prayer: God of David, you entrusted the governance of your people, Israel, to the hand of your servant, David. You stretched forth from Zion the scepter of his power, and he ruled in princely splendor. From his descendants you raised up Jesus, your servant and your Son, who through his cross, taught us that power consists of powerlessness. Make us true servants; form us into the image of Jesus, who lives and reigns with you and the Holy Spirit, one God, for ever and ever. Amen.

POWERLESS WIDOW

Mark 12:38-44

Scripture: "This poor widow tossed in more than all the others who contributed to the treasury. For they all gave from their surplus wealth, but she, from her poverty, has tossed in all that she had, her whole livelihood" (Mark 12:43-44).

Reflection: The last seven verses (58-44) of chapter twelve of Mark's Gospel bring to an end the continuous reading of this Gospel during the weekday cycle. For the remaining twenty-six weeks, Matthew and Luke will be read. The other sections of Mark's Gospel are read on other Sundays during Cycle B.

In the course of these last verses of chapter twelve, Jesus warns his hearers about the inappropriate behavior of the scribes. As has been seen in the previous verses, their teaching is appropriate, but their behavior is not in line with what Christian behavior should be.

Appropriate behavior is modeled by a poor widow. She, who is a societal outcast and powerless, deposits two small coins worth only a few cents into the Temple treasury. Jesus declares that she gives from her poverty. She is now even more powerless and dependent than she was before her meager (magnanimous?) donation. Like a child, the widow is dependent on others.

This appropriate behavior is contrasted to that of the scribes, who "like walking about in long robes and greetings in the mar-ketplaces, seats of honor in the synagogues and places of honor at banquets" (12:38-39).

The way of the authentic Christian, the authentic follower of Jesus, is through dependency, poverty, powerlessness, and disdain.

Meditation: In what ways do you resemble the scribes and the widow?

Prayer: God of widows, in your kingdom all values are reversed: you uphold dependency, poverty, powerlessness, and disdain. You condemn independence, riches, power, and honor. Mold us into the image of your Son, Jesus, who though independent became dependent, though rich became poor, though powerful became powerless, though honorable became dishonored on the cross. We ask this through the same Jesus Christ, our Lord. Amen.

GENTILES IN STARLIGHT
Matthew 2:1-12

Scripture: When Jesus was born in Bethlehem of Judea, in the days of King Herod, Magi from the East arrived in Jerusalem asking, "Where is the newborn king of the Jews? We saw his star rising and came to worship him" (Matthew 2:1-2).

Reflection: Matthew's unique account of the visit of the Magi prepares the reader for Israel's rejection of Jesus and the Gentiles' acceptance of him. This is accomplished with a stroke of Matthean irony.

After narrating the birth of Jesus in Bethlehem of Judea, King David's home town, Matthew proceeds to inform the reader that Magi arrive in Jerusalem from the East. The East is a reference to Babylon, the city of Israel's 70-year captivity, which began in 587 B.C. The East calculated the calendar according to the stars, while the Jews determined the months of the year according to the phases of the moon.

Babylon, the city of darkness — from Israel's point of view — is contrasted with Jerusalem, the city of light in which God dwelt in the Temple. Matthean irony emerges in the story when the Magi, Gentile astrologers, declare that they have seen a star, which they understood to herald the birth of a "newborn king of the Jews" (2:2). However, after following the star to Jerusalem, the city of light, the star goes out until they leave the city! The city of light, as Matthew sees it, now lies in darkness.

The star motif also serves to ground the story in Old Testament messianic prophecy. In the book of Numbers, Balaam predicts that a "star shall advance from Jacob" (Numbers 24:17).

Jerusalem is also contrasted with Bethlehem. Bethlehem was located in the sticks; it was "Nowheresville." Yet, the Gentile Magi know that this is where the "newborn king of the Jews" must be. In order to stress the smallness of Bethlehem, Matthew, who is fond of quoting Old Testament texts to prove his point, freely employs a verse from the prophet Micah: "But you, Bethlehem-Ephrathah, so small that you are hardly named among the clans of Judah, from you shall I raise the one who is to rule over Israel; for his origin is from of old, from ancient times" (Micah 5:1).

There is also an allusion to a verse in the second book of Samuel. While David is being made king, the tribes of Israel remind him of what the Lord has said, "You shall be the shepherd of my people Israel and you shall be commander over them" (2 Samuel 5:2). Thus, Matthew emphasizes the messianic mission of Jesus.

The Magi who seek the child "worship him" (2:2), according to Matthew. The Magi themselves represent figures of great honor, but they come seeking one who is more honorable. They travel from the place of Israel's captivity to prostrate themselves and pay homage to a little child (cf. 2:11). Israel doesn't recognize who is in their midst. Israel believes that God is in the Temple in Jerusalem, while he is really lying in a manger in nearby Bethlehem!

By referring to the child as the "king of the Jews" (2:2), the Magi cause King Herod to be "greatly troubled, and all Jerusalem with him" (2:3). Herod is troubled because he considered himself to be king of the Jews. Yet, as Matthew sets the scene, the Magi worship the child and escape from Herod! A child's birth, according to Matthew, troubles the whole city. It is not until the end of the Gospel where the child, now adult, dies outside the city with a sign over his head declaring, "This is Jesus, the king of the Jews" (27:27) that the city begins to realize how troubling the child really was!

Furthermore, these Magi bring rather strange gifts to celebrate the birth of an infant. Their "gifts of gold, frankincense, and myrrh" (2:11) are usually presented to a family during a funeral and burial. Gold coins would have been placed over the eyes of the deceased; frankincense and myrrh would have been used to help cover the stench of decaying flesh. Matthew has gotten ahead of his own story and, in his own unique and ironic style, prepared the reader for the death of Jesus.

Meditation: When have you most recently realized that reality is not how you have always perceived it to be? What experience sparked your new perspective?

Prayer: God of Jews and Gentiles, you anointed your Son, Jesus Christ, as king of the universe. His coming as a man into the world shed new light upon your great love for your people. Teach us to recognize your presence in the irony of our lives. Make us faithful followers of Jesus, who lives and reigns with you and the Holy Spirit, one God, for ever and ever. Amen.

FEAST of the
BAPTISM
of the LORD

TO FULFILL ALL RIGHTEOUSNESS
Matthew 3:13-17

Cycle A

Scripture: Jesus came from Galilee to be baptized by John at the Jordan. John tried to prevent him, saying, "I need to be baptized by you, and yet you're coming to me?" But in answer Jesus said to him, "Let it be for now, for it is fitting for us to fulfill all God's will in this way" (Matthew 3:13-15).

Reflection: Matthew's source for the account of the baptism of Jesus (3:13-17) is Mark's Gospel (cf. Mark 1:9-11). However, he has expanded the narrative and reshaped it according to his own theological perspective. To understand what Matthew has done, the reader must be familiar with Mark's account of this event.

When Mark wrote his Gospel, he did not prefix it with an infancy narrative, as Matthew has done. In Mark, John the Baptist appears looking like Elijah, who was supposed to return to herald the coming of the Messiah, and then Jesus appears and is baptized — all within the first eleven verses of the first chapter of the Gospel!

The baptism of Jesus by John, as Mark portrayed it, caused something of a problem by the time Matthew was writing his Gospel. The question raised by Mark's account is this: If John baptized Jesus, who is the greater: John or Jesus? Some people were saying that the one who did the baptizing must have been the greater.

Another question raised by Mark's narrative concerns the identity of Jesus. The voice from the heavens, which is understood to be God, declares to Jesus, "You are my beloved Son; in you I am well pleased" (Mark 1:11). If God declares Jesus to be his Son at his baptism, who was he before the baptism? Also, it is important to note that according to Mark only Jesus hears the voice from the heavens and sees "the heavens torn apart and the Spirit descending upon him like a dove" (Mark 1:10).

Matthew attempted to answer the first question, which Mark's Gospel had raised, by portraying John as trying to prevent Jesus from having John baptize him. In Matthew, John says, "I need to be baptized by you, and yet you're coming to me?" (3:14). Jesus responds to John's question by ordering, "Let it be for now, for it is fitting for us to fulfill all God's will in this way" (3:15).

By adding this dialogue to Mark's account of Jesus' baptism, Matthew portrays Jesus as greater than John. This answers the first question raised by Mark's account of the baptism.

The scene also gives Matthew an opportunity to re-present one of his favorite themes — righteousness. Righteousness is doing or fulfilling God's will; it is behaving in the way that God wants. By being baptized by John, Jesus does God's will, according to Matthew.

Thus the author answers the second question about Jesus' origin by genealogy, a birth narrative, the Magi account, and the flight into and return from Egypt. By the time the reader gets to the end of chapter three, there is no doubt as to who Jesus is and from where he comes.

In fact, the voice from heaven no longer is addressed only to Jesus. In Matthew, God's declaration becomes a proclamation to the whole world: "This is my beloved Son in whom I am well pleased" (3:17).

Meditation: In which ways have you experienced God's proclamation that you are his beloved son/daughter in whom he is well pleased?

Prayer: Voice from the heavens, at the baptism of your Son, Jesus, you opened the heavens and poured out your Spirit upon him. Thus, he was anointed for the ministry of the proclamation of your kingdom to the whole world. On the day of our baptism, you shared the gift of the same Spirit with us and claimed us as your beloved sons and daughters. Keep us faithful to our mission. Help us to know your will and to do it. We ask this, Father, through our Lord Jesus Christ, your Son, who lives and reigns with you and the Holy Spirit, one God for ever and ever. Amen.

MY BELOVED SON

Mark 1:7-11

FEAST of the
BAPTISM
of the LORD

Cycle B

Scripture: As he was coming out of the water he (Jesus) saw the heavens torn apart and the Spirit descending upon him like a dove. And a voice came from heaven, "You are my beloved Son; in you I am well pleased" (Mark 1:10-11).

Reflection: Mark's account of Jesus' baptism is very short and occurs immediately after the preaching of John the Baptist, who declares, "One more powerful than I am is coming after me, the strap of whose sandals I'm not worthy to stoop down and untie. I've baptized you with water, but he'll baptize you with the Holy Spirit" (1:7-8). The baptism of Jesus with water occurs immediately; the baptism with the Holy Spirit occurs outside the story line of the Gospel; for Mark it represents what was going on in his community at the time he was writing this Gospel.

Jesus' baptism is a private affair in Mark. Only Jesus sees "the heavens torn apart and the Spirit descending upon him like a dove" (1:10). It is a private revelation for Jesus. It is an anointing scene, wherein Jesus is equipped for his ministry, which will consist of proclaiming, "The appointed time has come and the kingdom of God is at hand. Repent, and believe in the good news" (1:15).

Only Jesus hears the voice from heaven declare, "You are my beloved Son; in you I am well pleased" (1:11). For Mark, Jesus is a "divine warrior," who has no history before his baptism and who gets his title and mission when he is baptized.

However, Jesus is also a secret or hidden warrior. Only Jesus, the voice from heaven, and the reader know Jesus' true identity. Mark has set the stage for an interesting story of disciples — who attempt to discover Jesus' identity — and adversaries, who seem to know exactly who Jesus is.

Meditation: In which ways do you identify Jesus? Make a list of answers to the question, "Who is Jesus?"

Prayer: God of the heavens, you revealed the unique relationship with you of your Son, our Lord Jesus Christ, after his baptism in the Jordan River. You poured out on him your Spirit and sent him to proclaim that your kingdom is at hand. On the day of our baptism you poured out on us the same Holy Spirit and claimed us as your beloved sons and daughters. Strengthen our faith in your Gospel. Move us to repentance. Place the words of your good news on our lips that others may come to faith in Jesus, who lives and reigns with you and the Holy Spirit, one God, for ever and ever. Amen.

ANOINTED WITH THE HOLY SPIRIT

Luke 3:15-16, 21-22

FEAST of the
BAPTISM
of the LORD

Cycle C

Scripture: John the Baptist responded by telling everyone...
"He (Jesus) will baptize you with the Holy Spirit and fire"
... Now it happened that when all the people had been
baptized, and when Jesus had been baptized and was in
prayer, the sky was opened and the Holy Spirit descended
upon him in bodily form like a dove (Luke 3:16, 21-22).

Reflection: Luke's account of Jesus' baptism comes from Mark
(cf. 1:7-11). However, Luke has reshaped his Marcan source to
answer some questions which Mark's account of Jesus' baptism
had raised for his community and to conform it to his own theological perspective.

The first trace of Luke's pen on Mark's narrative can be
found in John the Baptist's words, "He will baptize you with the
Holy Spirit and fire" (3:16). The baptism with the Holy Spirit and
fire is a reference to Pentecost, which is narrated only by Luke in
his second volume, the Acts of the Apostles (2:1-4), of his two-
volume work.

The next trace that Luke left on Mark's original narrative of
the baptism of Jesus is found in his portrayal of Jesus at prayer
after he had been baptized (cf. 3:21).

Throughout the Gospel, Luke presents Jesus at prayer before important events in his ministry. Before he chooses the

Twelve, Jesus prays (cf. 6:12). Before Peter's confession of Jesus' identity, Jesus prays (cf. 9:18). Before the transfiguration, Jesus prays (cf. 9:28). Jesus prays before he teaches his disciples to pray (cf. 11:1), at the Last Supper (cf. 22:32), on the Mount of Olives (cf. 22:41), and on the cross (cf. 23:46).

With his narrative of Jesus' baptism, Luke also answers two questions which were raised by members of his community in response to Mark's Gospel. The first question concerned who was greater — John the Baptist or Jesus. If John baptized Jesus, some people had concluded that he must be the greater.

Luke answers this question by including an intricate birth prediction and infancy account of both John and Jesus. It is clear that Jesus will be and is the greater even before he or John is born.

To be sure that he had taken care of this question, Luke also portrays Herod as "putting John is prison" (3:20) before he says anything about Jesus' being baptized. Thus, after a careful reading of Luke's Gospel, the reader discovers that John didn't baptize Jesus, according to Luke, because he was in prison.

The other question that Mark's Gospel had raised concerned the origins of Jesus. According to Mark, Jesus simply came from Nazareth of Galilee. Before he appears in the Gospel, there is nothing said about his birth.

Luke's two long chapters, which present the announcement of Jesus' birth, the birth itself, and many other events surrounding his birth, leave no doubt as to who Jesus is even before he is born. Thus, the question of Jesus' origins is taken care of for Luke's community.

More than any other Gospel, Luke's Gospel portrays Jesus as God's servant and alludes to the prophet Isaiah, "Here is my servant, whom I uphold, my chosen one in whom I delight. I have put my spirit upon him" (Isaiah 42:1). Throughout the Gospel, Luke will portray Jesus as the anointed Son of God. Jesus, filled with the Holy Spirit, becomes the example of the authentic praying Christian in Luke's Gospel. Followers of Jesus, according to Luke, must imitate the beloved Son in whom the Father was well pleased.

Meditation: In which ways have you experienced the gift of the Holy Spirit through prayer?

Prayer: God of spirit and fire, you poured out the gift of your Holy Spirit on your Son after his baptism in the Jordan River. You sent the fire of your Spirit upon his first disciples to strengthen them in bearing witness to Jesus' message of the presence of your kingdom. Open the heavens and let your Spirit descend upon us. Baptize us with the fire of your mission that we may proclaim the good news of Jesus throughout the world. We ask this through our Lord Jesus Christ, who lives and reigns with you and the Holy Spirit, one God, for ever and ever. Amen.

FEAST of the
PRESENTATION
of the LORD

DESTINED FOR THE
FALL AND RISE OF MANY
Luke 2:22-40

February 2

Scripture: Simeon blessed them (Joseph and Mary) and said to Mary his (Jesus') mother, "Behold, this child is destined to bring about the fall and rise of many in Israel, and to be a sign that will be opposed (and a sword will pierce your own soul,) so that the thoughts of many hearts may be revealed" (Luke 2:34-35).

Reflection: The Feast of the Presentation of the Lord is based on Luke's unique account of the presentation of Jesus in the Temple (2:22-40), which occurs after his circumcision and naming (2:21) and before another unique narrative about his being lost in the Temple (2:41-52). Luke's source for this material is the Old Testament, especially the account of Hannah's presentation of Samuel (cf. 1 Samuel 1:24-28). Luke also has in mind the Exodus stipulation of consecrating the first born son to the Lord (cf. Exodus 13:2, 12). The author's real interest in narrating this story is to prepare the reader for events which will take place later in the Gospel and to present some of the themes which he will develop throughout the Gospel.

Simeon, a man who "was upright and devout, who awaited the liberation of Israel" (2:25), and Anna, an old woman who "never left the Temple, but worshiped night and day with fasting and prayer" (2:37), represent those Jews who recognized Jesus to be the Messiah. Luke tells the reader, "It had been revealed to (Simeon) by the Holy Spirit that he would not see death before he saw the Messiah of the Lord" (2:26). Anna "gave thanks to God and spoke about the child to all who were awaiting the liberation of Jerusalem" (2:38).

Luke is saying that Jesus is the fulfillment of the hopes of Israel. He is the Messiah, for whom the people waited. He is the one who establishes God's rule, God's kingdom. Those, like Simeon and Anna, who are filled with the Holy Spirit, recognize Jesus as the Messiah. Throughout the Gospel, Luke will introduce the reader to those who recognize Jesus as Messiah and those who do not.

Jesus' proclamation of the presence of God's kingdom will cause "the fall and rise of many in Israel" (2:34). The Pharisees and scholars of the law, who were considered to be on the top rung of the ladder in Israel, will fall, while the tax collectors and sinners, who were considered to be below the bottom rung of the ladder, will rise. Indeed, Jesus is "a sign that will be contradicted" (2:34).

Obedience to the law and will of God is an important Lucan theme, which is begun in the narration of Jesus' presentation in the Temple and carried on throughout the Gospel. Joseph and Mary act "according to the law of Moses" (2:22), "just as it is written in the law of the Lord" (2:23). They act in "accordance with the dictate in the law of the Lord" (2:24).

The ministry of Jesus will be one of fulfilling the will of God.

Luke also introduces the theme of Jesus' significance for all people. Jesus is not just the "glory of Israel" (2:32), but he is also "a light of revelation to the Gentiles" (2:32). The mission to the Gentiles is important to Luke, because by the time of his writing of his Gospel, the message of Jesus was being preached to the Gentiles, and they were accepting it. This author portrays Jesus' ministry to the Gentiles in the Gospel, but he saves his description of the major mission for the Acts of the Apostles, volume two of his two-volume work.

Meditation: In which ways have you recognized the presence of God in your life, like Simeon and Anna recognized Jesus as the Messiah?

Prayer: "Now you send your servant away in peace, O Master, according to your word, because my eyes have seen your salvation, prepared in the presence of all the peoples, a light of revelation to the Gentiles, and glory to your people Israel" (Luke 2:29-32). Amen.

SO MUCH LOVE
John 3:16-18

SOLEMNITY
of the
HOLY TRINITY
First Sunday after Pentecost

Cycle A

Scripture: God so loved the word that he gave his only begotten Son, so that everyone who believes in him will not die but will have eternal life (John 3:16).

Reflection: This section of John's Gospel (3:16-18) is part of the unique Johannine dialogue between Nicodemus and Jesus.

After discussing the meaning of "being born from above" (3:3), Jesus explains that "just as Moses lifted up the serpent in the desert, so must the Son of Man be lifted up, so that everyone who believes in him may have eternal life" (3:14-15).

God's love for the world motivated God to give his only Son, "so that everyone who believes in him will not die but will have eternal life" (3:16). As usual, John's choice of words indicate a multiplicity of meanings. God's giving of his Son refers both to the incarnation and to his being "lifted up" (3:14) in death on the cross. All of Jesus' life was a gift to people from God.

God's gift of Jesus was for the purpose of eternal life, which does not so much refer to an infinitude of life as, rather, to a quality of new life. The way to share in eternal life is through faith in Jesus, who came to save, to motivate people to believe.

John makes it clear that "God did not send his Son into the world to condemn the world, but that the world might be saved through him" (3:17). In other words, God did not set up the people of the world. Jesus did not function as judge, nor did he condemn

anyone. His coming into the world, however, did provoke judgment — human if not divine.

"Whoever believes in him will not be condemned, but whoever does not believe has already been condemned, because he
hasn't believed in the name of the only begotten Son of God"
(3:18). For John, judgment consists of not believing in Jesus as
the Son of God. Those who do not believe have judged themselves. A deliberate refusal to believe in Jesus results in self-condemnation, according to John.

The focus of this section of John's Gospel is on the vastness
of God's love for the world, and not on God's desire to condemn
the world. Jesus manifests God's love. He offers eternal life, salvation, to those who believe. Only self-condemnation awaits
those who refuse to believe.

Meditation: In which ways have you experienced the unlimited
love of God?

Prayer: God of love, you so loved the world, that you gave your
only Son, Jesus Christ, in the mystery of the incarnation. He
manifested the limitless dimension of your love by being lifted
up on the cross, and thus he demonstrated that you did not wish
to condemn the world but to save it. Strengthen our faith in the
name of your Son. Do not let anyone perish but bring all people
to the joy of your kingdom, where you live and reign with Jesus
and the Holy Spirit, one God, for ever and ever. Amen.

WITH YOU ALWAYS

Matthew 28:16-20

SOLEMNITY
of the
HOLY TRINITY
First Sunday after Pentecost

Cycle B

Scripture: "All authority in heaven and on earth has been given to me. Go, therefore, and make disciples of all nations... I'll be with you all the days until the end of the age" (Matthew 28:18-20).

Reflection: The last scene in Matthew's Gospel is the commissioning of the disciples (28:16-20). Not only is this narrative unique to this Gospel, but it functions as the second of the two bookends, the first of which was presented in the first chapter of the Gospel.

Matthew narrates that "the eleven disciples went into Galilee, to the mountain to which Jesus had directed them" (28:16). There are only eleven disciples because Judas, according to this author, had "hanged himself" (27:5). They gather on one of Matthew's favorite places — a mountain. Throughout the Gospel, the author has been interested in portraying Jesus as a new Moses. The first sermon delivered by Jesus takes place on a mountain. Jesus delivers four more sermons to bring the total to five, the same number of volumes in the Pentateuch, the traditional book of Moses.

Furthermore, ancient peoples believed that God lived on a mountain. Moses had gone up to the mountain to get the law, the Torah. Elijah had heard the tiny whispering voice of God on the mountain. Now, Jesus gives his farewell discourse to his disciples on a mountain. When the disciples saw him,"they worshiped him, but some were doubtful" (28:17). Faith is never as strong as it should be, according to Matthew. People always have "little faith" (6:30).

But even with "little faith" the disciples are sent forth on mission by Jesus, who, after his resurrection, possesses "all authority in heaven and on earth" (28:18). The mission is universal. They are to "make disciples of all nations" (28:19), a reference to both Jews and Gentiles, who have been one of Matthew's concerns since the initial story about the Magi from the East. They are to baptize "in the name of the Father, and of the Son, and of the Holy Spirit" (28:19); that is, they are to initiate people into the Church by using the baptismal formula which was already common in Matthew's community. Baptism indicates a union between the one being baptized, the community, and the Blessed Trinity.

Finally, the disciples are to teach people "to observe all" (28:20) that he has commanded them. Just as Matthew began the Gospel with a genealogy which demonstrates how God often reverses things, he so ends with an interesting reversal statement. Throughout the Gospel, Jesus never commands the disciples to do anything. He simply presents a new way of life for those who wish to follow him.

Then, the final sentence of the Gospel answers a question which was asked as early as chapter one, where the author indicated that the child's name was to be "'Emmanuel,' which means 'God is with us'" (1:23). Finally, the meaning of "Emmanuel" becomes clear when Jesus declares, "I'll be with you all the days until the end of the age" (28:20).

There is no Ascension scene in Matthew; there is no departure of Jesus into the heavens. He is Emmanuel; he is God present with his people. He will remain present until the end of the age. In this way, Matthew settles down for a long period of time between the commissioning of the disciples and the second coming of Jesus as judge, which he believes will happen some day. But this is not something to get excited about because God is with his people now.

Meditation: In which ways have you most recently experienced Jesus (God) being with you always?

Prayer: God of heaven and earth, you have established your presence among your people in the flesh and blood of Jesus, your Son. He has promised to remain with us, as we pilgrimage through life and make disciples of all nations. Keep us faithful to our mission. Remove our doubts. May we always worship you, Father, Son, and Holy Spirit, one God, who lives and reigns until the end of the age and for ever and ever. Amen.

TRUTH'S GUIDE

John 16:12-15

SOLEMNITY
of the
HOLY TRINITY
First Sunday after Pentecost

Cycle C

Scripture: "When he comes, the Spirit of truth, he'll lead you to the whole truth" (John 16:13).

Reflection: This section of John's Gospel (16:12-15) is taken from the author's unique discourse on Jesus' departure and the coming of the "intercessor" or "advocate" (15:26), the "Spirit of truth" (16:13) (cf. 15:26-16:15). According to John, there is much more that the disciples need to be told by Jesus, but they "cannot bear it now" (16:12). "Now" refers to the present.

The Spirit of truth is always at work guiding people "to the whole truth" (16:13). In other words, the Spirit moves people to recognize the truth about Jesus. Furthermore, "he will expose sin and righteousness and judgment to the world for what it is" (16:8).

According to John, sin is a person's refusal to believe in Jesus. Even though Jesus was condemned to death and crucified, he was righteous, that is, he behaved according to God's will. Therefore, he has triumphed over the ruler of this world — Satan — by his death and resurrection. The Spirit of truth clarifies these points.

What the Spirit reveals to the followers of Jesus, he receives from Jesus, who has a unique relationship with the Father. In John, Jesus declares, "Everything that the Father has is mine; that's why I said that he (the Spirit) will receive what is mine and proclaim it to you" (16:15).

The Spirit of truth continues to guide all of those who believe in Jesus. He will proclaim "the things that are to come" (16:13) not in the sense of predicting the future, but by interpreting for believers what Jesus has already said and done.

Meditation: In what recent experience have you discovered the Spirit of truth guiding you to the whole truth?

Prayer: Almighty God, you revealed your face when you completed the creation of the heavens and the earth and formed man and woman in your own image and likeness. You revealed your love for people when you sent your incarnate Word to show your people how to live. You revealed your truth with the gift of your Spirit. Mold us into the image of Jesus that we may follow his way of life and be guided by the Spirit of truth. We ask this of you, Father, Son, and Holy Spirit, who live and reign, one God, for ever and ever. Amen.

SOLEMNITY
of the
BODY and BLOOD
of CHRIST
Second Sunday after Pentecost

Cycle A

LIVING BREAD

John 6:51-58

Scripture: "I am the living bread that came down from heaven. Anyone who eats this bread will live forever. The bread that I'll give for the life of the world is my flesh" (John 6:51).

Reflection: This section of John's Gospel (6:51-58) is part of the multiplication of the loaves and the ensuing bread of life discourse (cf. 6:1-71). It reflects the author's theological understanding of the Eucharist. He teases the reader into seeing his perspective by his use of words which are laden with multiple meanings.

In this passage, Jesus claims that he is the "living bread that came down from heaven" (6:51). "Living bread" means that Jesus, God's gift to the world, is alive after his death and resurrection, that is, now, and that "anyone who eats this bread will live forever" (6:51), that is, will share in Jesus' resurrected, or eternal life. In order to share eternal life, a person must eat the "living bread," Jesus' "flesh" (6:51), which he has given on the cross "for the life of the world" (6:51).

The Jews, John's favorite word for anyone who does not understand what Jesus is talking about, ask, "How can this man give us (his) flesh to eat?" (6:52). They understand eating flesh in terms of cannibalism. John is using flesh in a sacramental way. "Unless you eat the flesh of the Son of Man and drink his blood, you do not have life within you. Whoever feeds on my flesh and drinks my blood has eternal life, and I will raise him (or her) up on the last day" (6:53-54).

According to John, Jesus' "flesh is true food" (6:55), that is, that which sustains life. And his "blood, true drink." Drinking blood was as repulsive as eating human flesh to the Jews. Blood was considered to be the source of the body's life. When someone bled, he or she was losing his or her life. For Jesus to declare that "his blood is true drink" (6:55) means that Jesus is the source of eternal life.

Those who eat the flesh of Jesus and drink his blood remain in him and he in them (cf. 6:56). There is an intimate communion between them and Jesus. This union is so close that the flesh and blood of Jesus are commingled with the flesh and blood of his people.

There is another parallel. "Just as the living Father sent me, and I live because of the Father, so too, whoever feeds on me will live because of me" (6:57). The life that Jesus has received from God is now available to anyone through the Eucharist. All one has to do is to feast sacramentally on the body and blood of Jesus, "the bread that came down from heaven" (6:58).

In the desert after the great escape from Egypt, the Israelites were fed manna, bread from heaven. However, they ate this bread and they died. Jesus is bread for eternal life. "Anyone who eats this bread will live forever" (6:58).

Meditation: Make a list of all the different staples of life, kinds of human work, various fruits of the earth, and so forth, you can think of. How do these apply to Jesus?

Prayer: Father, once you fed your people with manna in the desert, but they died nonetheless. In the fullness of time, you sent your Son, Jesus, the living bread that came down from heaven. He has promised us that if we eat this bread we will live forever. Give us the true flesh and the true blood of Jesus that we may be filled with life and be raised up on the last day. We ask this through our Lord Jesus Christ, who lives and reigns with you and the Holy Spirit, one God, for ever and ever. Amen.

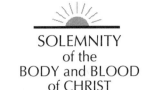

SOLEMNITY
of the
BODY and BLOOD
of CHRIST
Second Sunday after Pentecost

Cycle B

THE BLOOD OF
THE COVENANT

Mark 14:12-16, 22-26

Scripture: While they were eating, he (Jesus) took bread, blessed it, broke it, and gave it to them (his disciples) and said, "Take it; this is my body." And taking the cup, he blessed it and gave it to them, and they all drank from it. Then he said to them, "This is my blood of the covenant, which will be poured out for many" (Mark 14:22-24).

Reflection: The narrative about the preparations for the Passover (14:12-16) and the Lord's Supper (14:22-26) are part of Mark's passion account, which begins with the conspiracy against Jesus, the anointing at Bethany, and Judas' plot to betray Jesus (14:1-11). The narrative is divided by Jesus' prediction of Judas' betrayal (14:17-21), and it is followed by Jesus' prediction of Peter's denial (14:27-31).

The narrative about the preparations for the Passover (14:12-16) comes from the same cycle or type of oral tradition as the narrative of Jesus' entry into Jerusalem (11:1-11).

Both contain preparation by the disciples, predictions by Jesus, and fulfillments of the predictions. The placement of the narrative about the Lord's Supper (14:22-26) illustrates Mark's interest in the connection between Passover, the Eucharist, and betrayal.

Passover was the annual remembrance and celebration of

Israel's release from Egyptian slavery during the night. It began at sunset after the Passover lambs had been sacrificed in the Temple. The Feast of Unleavened Bread was joined to Passover at an early date to commemorate Israel's affliction in Egypt and the haste with which the nation left the land of slavery. By remembering the past events of salvation, the people looked forward and hoped for deliverance from their then-present domination by the Romans.

The practice of the early followers of Jesus of celebrating the Eucharist has been woven into this narrative by Mark. The words of blessing for the bread, "Take it; this is my body" (14:22), and the words of thanks for the cup, "This is my blood of the covenant, which will be poured out for many" (14:24), reflect a liturgical formula of the early Church.

The emphasis of this formula is on the absence of Jesus. "Amen, I say to you, I shall not drink again of the fruit of the vine until the day when I drink it new in the kingdom of God" (14:25). The early Church remembered Jesus by breaking bread and drinking wine; it celebrated his absence, while waiting for his coming in glory.

Also, Mark does not understand Jesus' death as beginning anything new. His blood is that "of the covenant" (14:24); only Luke makes Jesus' action a "new" covenant. Jesus' death is a continuance and perfection of the covenant which Moses sealed in blood between the Israelites and God (cf. Exodus 24:1-8).

The placement of the Lord's Supper between the prediction of the betrayal of Judas and the prediction of the denial of Peter by Mark serves to illustrate the author's theological understanding of Jesus' death. For this writer, God is found in betrayal and denial which results in suffering and death.

Not only do Judas and Peter betray Jesus, but all the disciples "left him and fled" (14:50). He is abandoned by everyone and must face rejection, suffering, and death all alone. On the cross he voices the depth of abandonment, when he cries, "My God, my God, why have you forsaken me?" (15:34). It is at the moment of death that Jesus is most human and experiences the depths of being alone, abandoned. For Mark, this is exactly where God is found.

Therefore, every time that followers of Jesus gather together to break bread and to drink wine in his memory, they do so like the Israelites of old; that is, they remember his great deeds of the past and they look forward with hope to his coming in glory. They celebrate his death — his abandonment, his betrayal — as they come to realize that when they are most human, like Jesus, it is then that they have truly discovered God.

Meditation: In which experiences of betrayal, abandonment, or suffering have you discovered the presence of God?

Prayer: God of Jesus, once you freed your chosen people from Egyptian slavery through the blood of the lamb, which was smeared on their doorposts. With Moses you sealed your covenant with your people through blood, which was sprinkled upon them and your altar. Through the blood of Jesus, you declared your presence in the betrayal, abandonment, suffering, and death of your Son on the cross. When we celebrate the Eucharist of Jesus, remind us of his lesson, as we wait for his coming in glory. He lives and reigns with you and the Holy Spirit, one God, for ever and ever. Amen.

SOLEMNITY
of the
BODY and BLOOD
of CHRIST
Second Sunday after Pentecost

Cycle C

TAKE, BLESS, BREAK, GIVE

Luke 9:11-17

Scripture: The crowds... followed him (Jesus). After greeting them he spoke to them about the kingdom of God and cured those who were in need of healing... Then he took the five loaves and the two fish and, after looking up to heaven, he blessed them and broke them into pieces and kept giving them to the disciples to distribute to the crowd (Luke 9:11, 16).

Reflection: Luke's account of the feeding of the five thousand comes from Mark's Gospel (cf. 6:30-44); however, this author has reworked the narrative to fit his own theological perspective on the Eucharist. In Luke's community, the Eucharist is the extension of the multiplication of the loaves and the fishes and of Jesus' last meal with his disciples. It is the way that the fellowship meals of Jesus are extended to the Church. Those who gather for this meal remember Jesus' martyrdom.

Luke portrays Jesus as feeding the crowd with the Word before he feeds them with bread and fish. Jesus "greeted them and spoke to them about the kingdom of God" (9:11). He also "healed those who needed to be cured" (9:11). Thus, Luke emphasizes the importance of hearing the word of God and acting on it.

This author is also interested in the role of the disciples. Before this scene they had been sent out on mission (cf. 9:1-6). Now, they were eager to dismiss the crowd so that they could "go to the surrounding villages and farms and find food" (9:12) but were told by Jesus to "give them something to eat" (9:13) themselves.

After blessing the loaves and the fishes, Jesus "kept giving them to the disciples to distribute to the crowd" (9:16). Throughout this narrative, Luke focuses on the role of the disciples after Jesus' death, when their mission is to continue to proclaim the word of God and to break the bread of Jesus. Luke illustrates this throughout the Acts of the Apostles, his second volume.

Jesus' act of "taking the five loaves and the two fish," "blessing them" and "breaking them into pieces," "giving them to the disciples to distribute to the crowd" (9:16) echo the four-fold liturgical action of the Eucharist of the early Church — taking, blessing, breaking, and giving. This eucharistic formula is repeated in the Last Supper narrative (22:19) and in the narrative regarding Jesus' appearance to two of his disciples on the road to Emmaus (24:30).

For Luke, Jesus is the one who satisfies hunger. "The hungry he (the Lord) has filled with good things" (1:53), Mary proclaimed. Now, the reader begins to discover that the "good things" are the word and food of Jesus. "They all ate and were filled" (9:17), notes Luke. The author reinforces this point by locating this event in Bethsaida, which means "place of satisfaction." Also Jesus himself had proclaimed in Luke's version of the beatitudes, "Blessed are you who hunger now, for you shall have your fill" (6:21).

The author maintains Mark's numerical significance. There are "five loaves and two fish" (9:13), which add up to seven, a sign of completion. Also, when "they picked up what was left over" they had twelve baskets of fragments (9:17). Twelve refers to the twelve tribes of Israel, with which God began a chosen people. Thus, Jesus completes the old covenant and he begins a new one, with a group of twelve disciples who are commissioned to gather in the harvest of the new people of God. It is with a little that God feeds many.

Meditation: In which ways has God fed you during the past week?

Prayer: God of bread, Jesus, your Son, satisfied the hunger of the crowd by proclaiming your word and by breaking bread. He commissioned his followers to continue his action throughout the world. Give us the courage to make your name known to all people. Send us the Holy Spirit to unite us in taking, blessing, breaking, and giving the bread of Jesus to each other. Guide us to the kingdom, where you live and reign with Jesus and the Holy Spirit, one God, for ever and ever. Amen.